The 7 Secrets of
Motivating
& Inspiring
Your Team

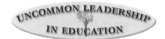

UNCOMMON LEADERSHIP
IN EDUCATION

The 7 *Secrets* of Motivating & Inspiring Your Team

BY BETTY HOLLAS

Crystal Springs
SDE BOOKS

a division of Staff Development for Educators
Peterborough, New Hampshire

Published by Crystal Springs Books
A division of Staff Development for Educators (SDE)
10 Sharon Road, PO Box 500
Peterborough, NH 03458
1-800-321-0401
www.SDE.com/crystalsprings

Published 2009
Printed in the United States of America
13 12 11 10   2 3 4 5

ISBN: 978-1-934026-21-2

Library of Congress Cataloging-in-Publication Data

Hollas, Betty, 1948-
   Uncommon leadership in education : the 7 secrets of motivating & inspiring
        your team / by Betty Hollas.
      p. cm.
   Includes index.
   ISBN 978-1-934026-21-2
   1. Educational leadership. 2. School management and organization. I. Title.

   LB2806.H645 2009
   371.2--dc22

                                        2008040968

Editor: Sharon Smith
Art Director and Designer: S. Dunholter
Production Coordinator: Deborah Fredericks
Illustrator: Mary Ruzicka

For Angelica

Contents

Acknowledgments

Thank you to:

Soosen Dunholter, designer and art director, who manages to combine clarity and creativity throughout these pages.

Sharon Smith, who is more than an editor. Sharon can take the copy I send her and turn it into something magical.

Deb Fredericks, Publishing Coordinator at Staff Development for Educators, for pulling all the pieces of the publishing process together.

Jim Grant, Executive Director of Staff Development for Educators, speaker, author, and friend; and Char Forsten, Associate Executive Director of Staff Development for Educators, speaker, author, and friend—both of whom continue to be endless sources of ideas, inspiration, and good times.

Angelica S. Frias, M.D., a special friend who read the manuscript and gave me great ideas and useful feedback.

Introduction

Let me introduce myself to you. My name is Betty. My entire career has been in education. First I was a teacher, then an assistant principal, and then a principal. Currently, I have the honor of working with teachers and administrators nationally and internationally as I travel all over the place giving workshops through Staff Development for Educators.

I also like to hear as much as I can of what other people have to say about education. Several years ago, when I attended a workshop on classroom management, the speaker made a big point of telling participants that you simply cannot motivate a student—that all motivation must come from within. I confess that my mind started to wander a little right about then. I wasn't so sure I agreed with the speaker on that particular point, and I started thinking about people in my life who had motivated me.

Pretty soon I was remembering the summer when my son was around eleven years old and his dad, sister, and I accompanied him to a baseball camp in Stillwater, Oklahoma. Now this camp was led by Gary Ward, the Oklahoma State University baseball coach, who was pretty famous at the time. The camp was five days long, and the plan was that my husband and son would attend the camp during the day while my daughter and I slept late, enjoyed the pool at the hotel, and so on. I decided to attend the camp the first morning, though, so I could be part of the orientation and learn firsthand about some of the experiences the kids would be having.

His enthusiasm and passion gave me more of a jolt than the coffee I was drinking.

I remember it was very early when Coach Ward approached the bleachers where all the campers and their families were gathered, but when he started talking, his enthusiasm and passion gave me more of a jolt than the coffee I was drinking. He was so excited so very early in the morning about what was going to be happening during the week. The excitement he exhibited reeled me in and made me pay attention to his words and his message. Before he finished, he told the campers that each day would start the same way, with a motivational talk.

I could not get his words and his excitement out of my head for the rest of the day. In fact, I decided I needed to hear this guy speak *every* morning. So I decided to forgo my plans to sleep late. Instead, I got up (and dragged my daughter out of bed) with my husband and son each morning that week so that I could hear Coach Ward's twenty-minute motivational talk. He was definitely motivating *me*! He had an ability to channel the energies of others in a positive direction, inspiring and influencing them to do their best. Perhaps this is one of the reasons that under his leadership, OSU won several baseball conference championships and went to numerous College World Series.

What does this have to do with you? Well, think about your role as an educational leader. Yes, managing the staff, providing instructional leadership, and working on the culture of your school are important. But I'm suggesting to you that those roles are no longer enough. The challenges you face in today's society and schools are more complex than ever. In order to create the kind of school needed for today's students and today's society, I think you need to consider a new way of looking at your role.

Who Is an Educational Leader?

When I say "educational leader," I'm talking in broad terms. Throughout this book, I refer to the role of the principal, but these ideas are intended for anyone who is an educational leader or who aspires to be an educational leader. That includes not only principals but also assistant principals, teacher members of leadership teams, classroom teachers, literacy and math coaches, curriculum specialists, department chairs, and district office leaders.

I'd like you to think in terms of what I call *uncommon* leadership. What I'm suggesting is that just like Coach Ward or any inspiring person you have known, you have the ability to motivate, influence, and inspire those you lead. When a leader in today's schools uses that ability to inspire people to do their best, he or she gets the results that are needed. This kind of uncommon leadership—this appropriate use of the ability to motivate and inspire—is what sets the best leaders apart from the rest.

Okay, I know what you may be thinking. You may be thinking that certainly inspiration and motivation can't possibly be the keys to leadership in today's schools. After all, you know that there are so many other things to discuss. In an era of accountability, talking about leadership in this way may seem like a "soft" concern compared to the "hard" data of student achievement scores, adequate yearly progress, and so on. However, both the research and my own experience as a school principal have convinced me that your ability to steer the energies of those you lead in a positive direction is at the heart of successful school improvement. I'm not suggesting that the principal's roles as manager, instructional leader, and shaper of school culture are not critical, because they certainly are. However, I am asking that as you read this book, you consider why I think inspirational leadership is so critical for effective principals today.

I invite you to go on a journey with me as we look at what I consider to be the essential skills of uncommon leaders. This book isn't at all about superstar principals. It's about how you can focus on a relatively small number of "secrets" that will help you and the teachers you work with get into and stay in the optimal shape for working to the best of everyone's ability. It's about how you can help teachers to help all students succeed.

The ideas I'll present aren't rocket science, and they may be familiar to you. So why do I call them secrets? Well, sometimes we completely lose sight of these really important concepts. We forget about them because our everyday lives as educational leaders are so hectic. And maybe we also forget about them because some of the skills they call for may not be so easy to learn. Sometimes, too, these ideas call for changing behavior, and that can be difficult.

However, the good news is that you *can* learn these skills. You *can* put these ideas into practice. And if you do that, you can inspire those you lead to make a greater effort than they ever would have even considered without you. And that's the *real* secret of successful leadership.

So . . . turn the page, and let's get going!

Secret #1

Nancy & the Green Cabinet:
The Power of Listening

It was the summer of 1998, and I was on cloud nine. I always enjoy anticipating a new school year, and while each year brings the excitement of a new beginning, this one was extra special for me. I was opening a brand-new school and was going to serve as its principal. So much made that opportunity truly special, but one of the best parts was that I got to hire the entire staff. Yes, you got it: hire the entire staff! The school was built to accommodate the growth in a community north of Houston, Texas, called The Woodlands. Because the area was, and still is, a very desirable place to live, work, and raise a family, it was growing rapidly. As a result, the school district, Conroe Independent School District, was opening new campuses frequently. No students were being transferred to the new school, and so no teachers were being transferred either. Therefore, I single-handedly interviewed and hired the entire staff for the opening year.

What made that particular aspect of the job even more exciting was that I was able to take several teachers with me from the school where I had been serving as principal. One of the teachers I chose to go with me was a first-grade teacher named Nancy. Nancy was the first-grade teacher every parent wanted his child to have—the one who had exactly the warmth and skills that make a great teacher for that all-important first-grade year. I was so glad that she'd agreed to come to the new school with me, and she was as excited as I was.

Part of what had all of us so thrilled was the new school building itself. When this building was constructed, it was equipped with the latest in technology; the latest in interior-design colors; built-ins and furniture to die for; and an exterior that you'd notice when you drove by. In short, this new building was equipped to the hilt and physically beautiful inside and out. Everyone was so excited to be moving into this bright new physical plant.

At the last minute, Nancy rushed into my office. She looked panic-stricken. I thought maybe something tragic had happened in her family.

One day I was waiting at my old school, along with the teachers who were moving with me, for the maintenance crew from the district to arrive and start loading all the boxes we had packed to take to the new school. At the last minute, Nancy rushed into my office. She looked panic-stricken. "What's the matter?" I asked. I thought maybe something tragic had happened in her family. She was near tears as she pleaded, "Betty, I need the maintenance crew to pack the green cabinet in my room. It has to go with me to the new school."

"What?" I had to laugh as I answered her. "Nancy, you have to be kidding me! That lime green cabinet"—and I mean really lime green—"can't possibly go to the new school. If anything, it should be thrown away. Not only will the lime green clash with the subtle earth tones of the new school, but it will look totally out of place surrounded by beautiful new built-ins! Why in the world do you feel you need to take that cabinet?"

I questioned her further, and then she really started to talk. She told me that the cabinet meant so much to her. She knew that she probably could pack the items it held, but that cabinet had been in her room all the years she'd been in the school. She said that she even loved the pencil sharpener that was attached to it—so many first graders over the years had used it to sharpen their brand-new, big fat pencils. It even had a hole in its wheel for those fat pencils.

At that point, I didn't bother to remind her that the new school had electric pencil sharpeners. You see, it was then that I realized this conversation was not really about that lime green cabinet. It was about Nancy. It was about her letting go of the tremendous success she'd had over the years at the old school and, in many ways, forging a new identity at the new school. It was change, the human side of change, and she was scared.

At that moment I had a choice. The path had forked, and I had to make a leadership decision. The choice was between what I call the "Human Doings" approach to leadership and the "Human Beings" approach.

The Human Doings approach would have been to tell Nancy that she absolutely could not take that cabinet with her. After all, my reputation as the leader of the new school was on the line. The community where the school was being opened was very affluent, and I had carefully considered how I would come across to the parents in that community. I had made special attempts to dress the right way and say the right things at all the parent and community meetings leading up to the opening. I had thought carefully about every decision regarding colors and decorations for the school. I also knew that real estate agents would be coming through the school all the time as they took prospective home buyers on tours of the beautiful new school their children would attend if they purchased a home in that school zone. And here was a teacher telling me that she needed to take an ugly old green cabinet and plop it in the middle of a brand-new first-grade classroom! "No way!" the Human Doings part of me was saying.

Well, guess what? I chose what I call the Human Beings approach. I told Nancy that she could take the green cabinet. She hugged me and thanked me and practically danced out of my office.

This conversation was not really about that lime green cabinet. It was about Nancy.

Anyone can take the Human Doings approach—get those scores up, narrow those achievement gaps, get those reports done. Anyone can lead a group to do the work (Human Doings). A slave master can do that. It takes an uncommon leader to influence and inspire those she leads to find meaning in their work, lives, and relationships so that they can be effective. That's what I mean by the Human

Beings approach. The uncommon leader helps others become whole human beings so that they can optimize their performance. As a leader, you want effective action. Therefore, your goal is to influence those you lead so that they can be effective. This is best accomplished not only through technical knowledge but also through emotional wisdom. In this case, I took the Human Beings approach to dealing with Nancy's concerns. I didn't downplay her emotional needs.

Believe me, at the time I wasn't so much doing that consciously. It was just that I had come to a fork in the path. I had to choose between the Human Doings way and the Human Beings way. I chose the Human Beings way mostly through sheer instinct. Somewhere inside myself, I realized at that moment that leadership is all about tapping into the energies and emotions of others, inspiring them to move in the right direction with enthusiasm and hope. It's about making others be better people and creating the conditions in which they can shine. This kind of uncommon leadership is what I think sets the best educational leaders apart from the rest. I am convinced that if you always opt for the Human Beings way of leadership, you will never go wrong.

The Human Doings Approach

The leader who takes the Human Doings approach ends up with a day that's caught up in the "stuff" of being principal. You know what I'm talking about: attending endless meetings, examining test data, observing in classrooms, dealing with discipline issues. Don't get me wrong; all of these things are important. Yet it's not a good idea to fall into this style of leadership exclusively. The Human Doings leader may think about helping others get into and stay in the optimal shape for working to the best of their abilities, but she knows that doing that takes time and energy. She thinks of the Human Beings approach as "dessert," not part of the main meal. She just can't find room for it on her already full plate. The Human Doings version of leadership is more about being the boss in charge of getting those lagging test scores up.

The Human Beings Approach

The Human Beings approach means finding ways not only to deal with the "stuff" of being principal but also to inspire and enable others to do excellent work and realize their potential. The Human Beings way of leadership is not so much about being the boss as it is about caring for people and creating a place where others can do their best work. It's an approach that can build successful, enduring schools.

> The Human Beings way of leadership . . . is about caring for people and creating a place where others can do their best work.

If you, like me, are a fan of Michael Fullan, you probably have read some of his work on the subject of change. In *The Six Secrets of Change*, Michael Fullan writes that the first secret is to "love your employees." He explains this using an example from education. I found it so interesting that he uses the piece of legislation that you're very familiar with—No Child Left Behind—and its implication that children always come first.

Now if you know the work of Michael Fullan, you know that he has always been a champion of the "moral imperative," as he calls it, of closing the achievement gap and raising the bar for all students. However, in *The Six Secrets of Change*, he suggests that the concept of always putting children first is both misleading and incomplete. He argues, using several examples, that we must love our employees just as much as we do our other stakeholders (the children and parents).

He then goes on to write that "one of the ways you love your employees is by creating the conditions for them to succeed" (Fullan 2008, 25). "Aha!" I thought as I read that. "That's the uncommon leader. That's the Human Beings approach!"

In the following chapters, I'll talk more about Human Doings vs. Human Beings. But for now, let's continue our exploration of uncommon leadership by focusing on the first important secret of a Human Beings leader. Let's talk about the power of listening.

Tips for Listening
Shut Up & Listen

There was a country song a few years ago titled "Shut Up and Kiss Me." Here's a new song title for you to put in the back of your mind and hum to yourself as you go through the day. The song is "Shut Up and Listen." Get in the habit of humming it all the time. You see, each and every day presents you with many situations that call for understanding the emotions of those you lead. When you understand where people are coming from, it's easier to consider the Human Beings approach. The way you do that is by studying other people's needs.

We spend a lot of time talking *at* teachers and not really asking questions and listening to what they're saying. We don't inspire others to go in the direction we want them to by ordering them to do what we say. Think of Nancy. The only reason I was able to respond with a Human Beings approach was that after I asked a question ("Why do you want to take that green cabinet?"), I was able to listen to her as she answered (and answered and answered).

My husband represents investors who want to buy companies. His job is to find companies that might be good matches for the investors he represents and that are owned by people who might consider selling. He looks for privately owned, medium-size companies—ones the owners have built from the ground up and are emotionally invested in. He told me that for the first few years, he spent too much time trying to convince the owners to sell and too little time helping the owners recognize that they might *want* to sell. He found that when he heard their stories and really studied their needs, that information helped him get them to consider selling. He learned that the best way to study their needs was to listen and ask questions. These days the first question he asks an owner is "What is your situation, and what would you like to do?"

As you work with teachers, make it a habit to find out everything you can about them: what they like to do; what is important to them; what they fear, love, and hate; what their aspirations are. You will stand a better chance of getting what you want out of those you lead if you first find out what *they* want. This is done through shutting up, asking questions, and listening. If you listen long enough, you will find out how to take the Human Beings approach with those you lead.

Here's a puzzle for you: can you take all the letters in the word "listen" and make another word that sums up what this tip is all about? Try it.

Answer to the puzzle: The word is "silent." Maybe there is a reason each letter in the word "silent" is also in the word "listen." Think about that!

Turn Off Your Blackberries, Blueberries, Cranberries & Other Distractions

Multitasking their way through the day is the norm for many principals unless they want to leave school at 10:30 or 11:00 at night. (I know that you may stay that late anyway.) But consider this: all that multitasking can be costly. When you temporarily shift your focus, even for only a couple of minutes to answer an e-mail or take a phone call, you increase the time it takes to finish the task you left—sometimes by as much as 25 percent (Schwartz 2007). A better way to manage your tasks might be to quit doing so much multitasking and to fully focus for a set amount of time on one activity before going on to the next one.

This can pay off for you personally, and it can pay off with your staff. I remember that at that new school I opened, we were so high-tech that we had every gadget known to man. Yet sometimes I felt as if we had every *distraction* known to man. Often when I was talking with a teacher in my office, I would interrupt our conversation to respond to a beep on my pager or to take a phone call. I really wasn't modeling the critical role of listening when I did that.

You know what stopped me? The look on one teacher's face when, in the middle of our conference, I took a call. I will never forget it: she looked devastated. I decided right then and there that I would never do that again. I decided that whenever anyone was talking to me, I would devote my full attention to that person. To pull that off, I had to force myself to get some sort of ritual going. So I decided to check my e-mail only twice a day—once in the morning and once in the evening before I left school. That was hard to do, because I was addicted to e-mail. (I certainly didn't want to miss out on anything.) Yet it paid off in more quality time with others, and I actually got more done.

The Three R's: Recognition, Rewards & Rituals

An important corollary to listening to your staff is *showing* them that you're listening—and really paying attention. Here are some simple but effective ways to do that.

- Pass out paychecks to teachers instead of putting them in teachers' mailboxes. When giving a paycheck to a teacher, personally thank him for his hard work.

- Give each teacher a certificate of time. The certificate is good for three hours of your time teaching the recipient's class anytime during the school year.

- Keep note cards handy and follow a schedule for writing a positive note to each staff member on a regular basis. Start your notes with "While I was in your classroom, I saw . . ."

- Use candy to create a reward. For example, periodically pass out candy with a motivational message. You might give each person a PayDay candy bar with a note that says, "You deserve an extra payday." Or a Milky Way bar with a note that says, "You are out of this world. Thanks for what you do." Or a Mounds bar with a note that says, "Thanks for the mounds of work you do." Think of the possibilities!

- Institute a ritual of providing food at faculty meetings. Food is always a welcome treat, and it certainly helps get people to show up on time!

- Host a monthly "Breakfast of Champions" for the staff. Either cook it yourself or have it catered, but either way, serve it yourself to staff members.

- Host a monthly "Whine and Cheese Reception." Offer teachers the opportunity to air their concerns, then truly listen to them. (The key to this isn't the whining. It's the listening—followed by an attempt to come up with a constructive solution together.)

A Tool for Listening

IN & OUT LISTENING

Purpose:

Part of what the uncommon leader does is to give teachers the knowledge and skills they need in order to be effective when working on a team. Sometimes structures such as common planning times or professional learning communities aren't enough. The purpose of this activity, which you can use with teachers, is to impress on them what a critical skill listening is in any kind of communication—whether it's listening to peers during a meeting of a professional learning community or listening to students in the classroom.

Materials:

Chairs arranged in circles of six

Time:

15–20 minutes

Procedure:

1. Participants sit in circles of six and identify themselves by calling out alternating letters: A, B, A, B, A, B.

2.   All the A's lean in toward the center of the circle, while the B's scoot out a bit, creating inner and outer circles.

3.   Give the A's a question to talk about for approximately four minutes. An example might be "What are some interventions that you've used in your classroom to help all students succeed?" The A's are to have a conversation among themselves as if no one else were listening.

4.   But of course the B's *are* listening. Their role is to take in everything the A's say and how they say it without talking or interrupting.

5.   The A's then lean out, and the B's lean in. Give the B's two minutes to report what they saw and heard. They may not judge or interpret—just report.

6.   The B's stay leaning in. They're about to respond to the same question that the A's responded to. However, the role of the listeners is about to change. Before the B's respond to the question, each A identifies out loud a specific B that he'll be listening to.

7.   The B's respond to the question for four minutes in the same way that the A's did—as if no one outside the group were listening. Each B knows who is focusing on her, but she does not address any comments to that person.

8.   After four minutes, each A stands up and tells his B what he thinks he heard B say.

Processing This Activity

Ask the participants in the whole group these questions:

- What did it feel like to be listened to carefully?
- Do you listen as well during the day to students, other staff members, and parents?
- Is listening important for a teacher?
- Could listening improve how well you do your job?

Challenge all participants to listen to others during the rest of the day as well as they did during this activity.

One More Note

Remember Nancy from the beginning of this chapter? A month into the school year at the new school, I looked up one day and saw Nancy in my office. With a sheepish grin, she asked if the secretary could do a maintenance order. I asked her what needed fixing when we were only a month into the school year at a brand-new school. She replied that nothing was broken. It was just that she wanted to have the green cabinet hauled away. She realized that she didn't really need it after all.

A Pearl to Ponder

People will forget what you say. They will forget what you do. But they will never forget how you made them feel.

—Carl W. Buechner

Secret #2

You Are the EGO:
Serving as an Emotional Guide for Others

Not long ago, I had an experience that really made me think. I'd been on the road working with teachers and administrators for most of the week, and I was waiting to catch the rental-car shuttle to the airport in Chicago. It was late on a Friday night, I was tired, and I was anxious to get home—and so were all the other "road warriors" who were waiting with me. No one was in a particularly good mood, including me.

That is, no one was in a good mood except the driver of the rental-car shuttle. He drove up to his waiting passengers, jumped out of the driver's seat, stood smiling before us, and said enthusiastically, "Great to see all of you. I'm here to serve you and give you a great ride over to O'Hare.

Let me help each of you with your bags. I know you're tired and have worked hard. My goal is to give you a great ride tonight."

I was shocked—first of all that he got off the bus and offered to help, but also that he was in such a chipper mood. There was no talk as we slowly and deliberately filed onto the bus, but when everyone was seated, the driver reached into a cooler next to his seat and asked if anyone would like a bottle of water. He told us he knew that we had worked hard and probably could use a cool drink. Several people took the water, and as it was being passed out, I noticed that passengers were beginning to talk to one another—something else that usually doesn't happen in that situation. As we departed, the driver told us that he had a vision—and he did use the word "vision." He told us that his vision was to get each of us to our particular terminal at O'Hare on time and safely and to make sure each of us had a pleasant and fun ride. (Yes, he used the word "fun.")

His vision was to get each of us to our particular terminal at O'Hare on time and safely and to make sure each of us had a pleasant and fun ride.

The driver started calling out names of states and asking us to respond according to where we were from. After about two minutes of this, the entire shuttle was buzzing with laughter and conversation. So there I was, thinking about this shuttle driver and leadership. (I am sort of obsessed with this stuff.) "Yes," I thought, "he is definitely an uncommon leader. He isn't just about the Human Doings way of leadership—herd them onto the bus, get them to the airport, herd them off, and do it again until the shift is up.

No, this driver is all about the Human Beings way of leadership—positively influencing the emotions of those he's leading [his passengers] with both his vision and his people skills at that moment."

I was so lost in my thoughts that I didn't even realize that I had blurted out loud, in front of everyone, exactly what I was thinking: "The climate is great in this shuttle tonight!" The lady next to me whispered, "Actually, I think it's a little chilly in here." I replied, "No, I wasn't thinking of that kind of climate." I went on to explain to her that I work with many educational leaders and that our driver certainly was exhibiting the kind of leadership skills that I've seen work so well in schools. He was driving the climate (the working environment of the group) in a positive direction, because he was what I call an uncommon leader—a Human Beings leader.

I could tell that she probably thought I was a little strange and that I was giving her more information than she wanted at that particular moment, but she did act interested, because by this point, all the passengers were acting interested in one another. By the time we reached our first drop-off point, people were saying good-bye to one another and wishing one another a safe flight—still more things that don't usually happen in these situations.

I was particularly interested in what the response to the driver would be. Passengers were thanking him. Some patted him on the back. Others told him that this was the best shuttle ride they'd ever had. One man asked how he could get in touch with the driver's supervisor to let him know how customer-friendly the man had been. I also noticed that the driver was getting nice tips—including the one I gave him as I said good-bye and thanked him for his "uncommon" hospitality.

The driver was our leader on that trip, and as the leader, he was the EGO—emotional guide for others. Because of

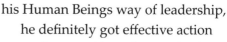

his Human Beings way of leadership, he definitely got effective action from us (those he was leading). He could have employed the usual Human Doings form of leadership that I've experienced with most of the rental-car shuttles I've taken. But if he'd done that, he probably wouldn't have gotten such effective action from us in terms of both interaction and tips.

I'm suggesting to you that as an educational leader, you, too, will get effective action from those you lead when you employ the Human Beings approach. You may not get the tips (monetary rewards) or all the positive attention from others that the shuttle driver did, but you will definitely be more likely to get some other rewards: more energy, enthusiasm, and commitment from those you lead. And all those things are important, because they in turn can lead to higher student achievement.

Let's consider this idea of a leader (whether on a rental-car shuttle, in an organization, in a school administration, or in a classroom) as an EGO—Emotional Guide for Others. What does being an emotional guide for others mean?

You have probably heard the term "emotional intelligence." In 1990, Peter Salovey and John Mayer came up with the term. Then in 1995, Daniel Goleman published a book called *Emotional Intelligence,* which he based on the work of Salovey and Mayer. Goleman's work popularized the concept of emotional intelligence. What he proposed was that the skills associated with emotional intelligence give people an advantage in areas such as leadership.

In Goleman's model, emotional intelligence means the ability to perceive and manage your emotions and those of others. Goleman's theory focuses on a crucial set of four capabilities within each individual: self-awareness (the ability to read your own emotions), self-management (mood management or the ability to control your emotions), social awareness (the ability to understand and react to the emotions of others), and social skills (the ability to inspire, influence, and develop others).

Goleman's Keys to Emotional Intelligence

- Self-awareness
- Self-management
- Social awareness
- Social skills

In 2006, Goleman published *Social Intelligence,* which he describes as a companion to *Emotional Intelligence.* In *Social Intelligence,* Goleman expands his theory of emotional intelligence and focuses on what happens when we connect with others. The most fundamental finding in *Social Intelligence* is that human beings are wired to connect. Goleman explains that each of us has a class of brain cells called "mirror neurons." These mirror neurons tune in to any person you are with and create in your brain a replica of the other person's emotions and actions—"mirrors" of how that person is feeling. In other words, you can catch someone's emotions just as you can catch a cold. I bet you can think of times when you've "caught" the emotions of someone else—both positive emotions and negative ones.

As an EGO or emotional guide for others, you have to have empathy. We touched on that earlier when we talked about Nancy. Empathy is a critical part of what Goleman considers emotional intelligence. However, true empathy means putting yourself in someone else's shoes while, at the same time, not "catching" that person's emotions.

For example, I remember a time when I was working with an extremely talented group of principals on a very important project. With this group's high level of competence, it was natural that as we discussed the details of the project, some competition might creep into the discussion—and that's exactly what I felt was happening. It was important for me to be able to empathize and understand why that might be happening, but also not to allow myself to participate in the competition. Doing so would have been a poor use of boundaries. We'll explore the concept of boundaries in leadership when we get to secret number 6. But for now, just know that proper boundaries can help you keep from catching unwanted emotions while still allowing you to be empathetic.

He then asked, "If all of this happened early this morning, why did you invite this difficult parent to dinner with us tonight?"

I remember a time when a very difficult parent yelled at me during a PTO board meeting early one morning. I walked around all day feeling angry. When I got home from school, my husband suggested that we go out to dinner. Wow! No cooking sounded great, except that when we arrived at the restaurant, I began telling my husband the entire story of what had happened at the PTO board meeting. The more I talked, the angrier I became. He finally stopped me and asked me what time all of this had occurred. I responded, "Around nine this morning." He then asked, "If all of this happened early this morning, why did you invite this difficult parent to dinner with us tonight?"

He had made his point. This person had gone through the entire day with me. She'd been given a ride home in my car, and she was eating dinner with us! I now understand what had happened: I had caught her emotions. In other words, I had picked up her feelings—after all, they were pretty strongly expressed—and had allowed her to ruin my day. The reason I had caught her emotions was that I had not been vaccinated against them. I had not maintained my boundaries.

My encounter with this parent had happened early in the morning, and there I was in the evening, still in a foul mood. Similarly, my experience with the rental-car shuttle driver left me feeling the pleasant effects of that trip even after arriving at the airport. It's important to remember that what you do can make someone else feel either better or worse, and that mood can stay with the person for a long time.

Another interesting finding from Goleman's work is that in a group setting, emotions ripple outward, with the strongest impact coming from the emotions of the most powerful person. Think about the implications of this. In the classroom, the most powerful person is the teacher. In the school, the most powerful person is probably you, the principal. Your style of interaction day in and day out can inspire, influence, and motivate others, or it can de-motivate and drain positive energy from them. This finding reinforces the need for educational leaders to be skilled in uncommon leadership—the Human Beings approach of managing one's own emotions and influencing the emotions of others in a positive way.

Even though this idea of connecting emotional intelligence or competence with leadership first became popular in the corporate world, it's now filtering into the world of education. Most of those who have done research in this field agree that although more research is needed, emotional skills are extremely valuable in the workplace. What I am suggesting to you is that by recognizing that you are an

EGO—emotional guide for others—you can put yourself in a better position to help your teachers fulfill their main mission: teaching!

Even though she's never been openly defiant with you, her body language speaks volumes. . . . And you know that she's pulling others in with her.

Let's consider a typical situation in a school and how you might deal with it. Let's say you have a young, first-year teacher in your building. She's doing a good job in her classroom with the students, but she seems to have an "attitude" when it comes to things outside the classroom walls. Even though she's never been openly defiant with you, her body language speaks volumes. Sometimes she rolls her eyes when you or others are talking about something she doesn't agree with. She talks with others about her views and seems to stir up discontent. Once in a while, you see her slam a door or throw a pile of papers down—all pretty good indications that she is angry about something. And you know that she's pulling others in with her. Ah, those mirror neurons. Others are catching her emotions! If you ignore this problem, it will probably lead to morale problems for others. What do you do as the EGO—the emotional guide for others?

The Human Doings Approach

One response might be to call the teacher into your office and chastise her—most likely by shooting from the hip. You might tell her that she's having a negative effect on the school environment and that you want her to explain what's bothering her.

If you do that, she'll probably deny that anything is wrong—and then after she leaves your office, she'll become even more disgruntled. This might result in your writing a letter expressing your disapproval and giving her a copy, indicating that it will also be placed in her personnel file.

But this approach probably won't solve the problem.

The Human Beings Approach

The uncommon leader knows something that many leaders do not know: it's a natural tendency for any follower to rebel against authority. This is particularly true for young teachers. Young teachers today typically do not have the respect for authority that educational leaders in years past could take for granted. They seem more willing to challenge the higher-ups. So the uncommon leader would realize that this teacher's behavior could be in part a result of this natural instinct to curb the leader's power (as well as her inability to deal with her anger directly).

The Human Beings way of dealing with this teacher might be to use some of the key emotional competencies of empathy, knowledge of how others behave, and impulse control (stifling that first impulse to angrily confront her—or to strangle her). When the teacher denies that anything is bothering her, you might suggest that the two of you meet again in about a week. You could tell her that even if nothing is bothering her, you'd like her feedback on how things could be improved at the school.

By handling the situation in this manner, you're indicating that there's a problem, but you're also setting things up so that she knows the meeting will not be confrontational. You might be influencing her behavior during the next week as well. Her behavior might improve, because now she knows that the next meeting won't focus on more complaints about her—you've already asked her for her feedback about potential improvements—and she doesn't want it to be uncomfortable. The most important thing you have done, however, is to use your emotional wisdom to reframe the situation. You've invited her to perceive her role not as a new and perhaps powerless teacher at the school, but rather as someone who can contribute and collaborate to make sure things function well. And that's the second secret of inspiring your team to greatness: influencing the emotions of each team member in a positive way.

Tips for Becoming an Emotional Guide for Others

Make Yourself Positively Contagious

I frequently visit the ATM located in the parking lot of my bank. For several years, the home screen gave me the instructions for making a transaction in a boring, command-and-control (Human Doings) kind of way. Then one day a couple of years ago, I noticed that the home screen had changed: it had a new, welcoming message. Now when I drive up, the screen greets me and asks if I'm having an outstanding day. As I go through each step, the screen encourages me and tells me I'm on the right track. At the end of the process, the screen thanks me, wishes me well, and expresses the hope that I continue to have an outstanding day. Service to others really seems to be the priority of that machine. That screen makes me feel as though I'm worth every penny I'm taking from it! I always drive away in a better mood than when I drove up.

It seems that the designers of that ATM understood that almost anywhere, including in front of an ATM, there is a vacuum just waiting to be filled by someone or something that can inspire and steer the energies of others in a positive direction. My question to you is, Could you be the ATM at your school?

What do I mean? You know I don't mean handing out 20-dollar bills! Here's what I'm suggesting. You probably would agree that working with some of the adults in your school can be a bit challenging. In fact, have you ever had the experience of driving into the school parking lot and getting into a foul mood just at the sight of their cars? You know the teachers I'm talking about. They're the ones who are probably in the teachers' lounge, indulging in a good meeting of what I call the BMW (bitch, moan, and whine) club. Those negative teachers think they have a license to spread that negativity around, and it can kill as surely as passive cigarette smoke. You ask them how they're doing, and they respond, "I made it. I'm vertical." You spend time around that, and pretty soon you're negative as well. At that point, you could easily fall into a Human Doings approach to the day.

So in the future, as you drive into the parking lot of your school each day, switch your thoughts to be like that home screen of the ATM. The minute you get out of your car, respond positively to everyone who greets you. When that person says, "Hi! How are you?" I want you to say "I am outstanding!" Just say it—even if you don't feel it at the moment. Those you lead need to see this positive passion modeled when they first see you every day. When teachers see you in action loving what you do, they will be more likely to impart a love of learning to their students.

You see, the uncommon leader is aware that *all* his moods—both good and bad—are contagious, and his goal is to spread his positive "germs" around.

Be a Finder

Sometimes when you assume the role of principal, it's easy to become more of a police officer than an educational leader. Because of the pressures of high-stakes testing and accountability, you can fall into the habit of micromanaging and becoming a watchdog over scores, benchmark assessments, and everything else. The uncommon leader, on the other hand, becomes a finder of strengths in those he leads and of ways to build on those strengths. The uncommon leader expects the best from others. When the people you lead know that you have confidence in them and that you expect great things from them, they're more likely to live up to your high expectations. If, on the other hand, you expect the worst, that's what you'll usually get.

For a number of years, I was the principal of Lamar Elementary School in Texas. Our mascot was the leopard. You have probably heard that a leopard never changes its spots. I can testify that that is not true, because I watched our "little Lamar leopards" change and grow every day. Each of those students developed and grew at his or her own rate, and the faculty knew it was important to recognize that.

Adopt that same attitude with your staff. Every group you lead will have a mixture of strengths and weaknesses. You have a choice—to focus and obsess on the weaknesses, or to focus and build on the strengths. When you make the effort to tap into the positive energy that each staff member possesses, you will help each one succeed. Nobody wants to fail. Let your teachers know that you believe in them and expect them to do well. If you do, they will be more likely to change their spots like the Lamar leopards.

Tools for Becoming an Emotional Guide for Others

PRAISE BEHIND YOUR BACK

Purpose:

This tool is a favorite of mine because it impresses two things on teachers. The first is the concept that everyone shares the responsibility for creating the right mood in a school. Everyone is responsible for boosting morale, for fostering conditions for collaborative work, and for influencing emotions in a positive way. The second concept it reinforces is the Human Beings belief that negativity about others we work with is not acceptable. In other words, the uncommon leader strives to create the understanding that it's going to take a lot of work to help all our students succeed. Therefore, getting sidetracked by gossiping behind people's backs has no place in the learning environment of a school. We don't have time for that, and negative gossip among staff members certainly does not help influence emotions in a positive way.

Materials:

>Chair; jar containing slips of paper, each with the name of a teacher; paper and pen or pencil

Time:

>Around 5 minutes at the end of a faculty meeting

Procedure:

1. Bring a chair to the front of the room, facing away from the group.

2. Pull a teacher's name out of the jar of names.

3. Ask the teacher to come to the front of the room with paper and pen and to sit in the chair.

4. Give the rest of the teachers one minute of "think time." Ask them to think of all the good things they could say about the person sitting in the chair.

5. Ask them to start calling out those good things. As they do, ask the teacher in the chair to write down everything he hears.

6. After a couple of minutes, ask everyone to stop. The teacher should have a long list of positive comments.

Processing This Activity

Ask, "Have we talked about the person in the chair behind his back?" The teachers will say, "Yes." Then remind them that the talk has all been positive. They will understand that the working norm is that if they're going to talk behind one another's backs, the talk must be positive.

HEADBANDS

Purpose:

>This activity, based on one by Linda Albert, illustrates how critical teachers' expectations and assumptions are as they relate to their students. When teachers expect more of their students, students begin to expect more of themselves.

Materials:

>Headbands you've created from sentence strips

Time:

10 minutes

Procedure:

1. Have each participant put on a headband without looking at what it says.

2. Once everyone is wearing a headband, instruct participants to stand up and move about the room pretending they are at a party and meeting as many people as they can. They are to decide how to treat each person based on the message on that person's headband.

3. After about 90 seconds, ask those who think they have positive messages on their headbands to stand on one side of the room and those who think they have negative messages to stand on the other side of the room.

4. Ask participants on both sides to share with the group as a whole some of the comments they received.

5. Ask participants to remove their headbands and see what the headbands say.

6. Point out to participants that in about 90 seconds, each of them could figure out whether she was getting a positive or a negative message from others. Ask them to think about the students they teach and the labels (headbands) those students come to school with each day.

7. Remind participants of the power they hold when they express (intentionally or not) expectations for their students. You might reinforce the point even further by sharing a quote like this one: "I'm not who I think I am. I'm not who you think I am. I am who I think you think I am." Or you could use this one: "Children will find in the eyes of teachers and parents who raise them mirrors in which they discover themselves."

8. Let teachers talk about headbands their students are wearing. Then have them discuss the impact of negative headbands and talk about what teachers can do to reverse that impact through focusing on the potential that lies in each student.

Suggestions for Headbands

Include both positive and negative labels on the headbands.
Here are some suggestions.

I am a leader.

I am capable.

I am creative.

I am athletic.

I like to read.

I am gifted.

I am intelligent.

I am self-confident.

I am computer-literate.

I am smart.

I am a role model.

I can be trusted.

I make good grades.

Everyone likes me.

I am confused.

I am bossy.

I am a klutz.

I am a slow learner.

I am insecure.

I am a failure.

I have a learning problem.

I am in special education.

I am a bully.

I am stressed-out.

I am invisible.

I am dyslexic.

I am ADHD.

GREETINGS THE 4-H WAY

Purpose:

By establishing this routine, you help students begin each day in a positive frame of mind for learning.

Materials:

None

Time:

Less time than it takes to complain about something

Procedure:

1. Ask teachers to greet students at the classroom door each day.

2. Suggest that they introduce students to the 4-H approach to morning greetings: As each student arrives, ask her, "How would you like to be greeted today?" Have the student indicate whether she'd prefer a hug, a handshake, or a high five. Or she can use the fourth "H" by coming up with some other response to the question, "How would you like to be greeted today?"

3. As students get used to the procedure, they'll know that the teacher will be there with a smile and an appropriate greeting every day.

Become the Greeter in Chief

If you want teachers to greet students the 4-H way every day, then you need to do that as well, because you are the role model. I used to do this. I would alternate spots for my greetings each morning. One day I would go to the back of the school, where the buses unloaded. As students got off the buses, I did the best I could to greet each and every one of them. Usually I would say something like "Good morning, Jack. I'm so glad you're here. I hope you have an outstanding day!"

The next day I would go to the front of the building, where bike riders, walkers, and students being dropped off by car entered the school. Often I would open the car door for students and greet them in the same way I greeted the bus riders.

I admit that some days I was really tempted to skip this ritual, because the minute I arrived at school, the Human Doings tasks were waiting. However, I would try as hard as I could not to deal with any of that until I had greeted the students. When I was able to take care of the greetings first, that routine set the tone not only for the students but for me as well. It was always my favorite part of the day.

A Pearl to Ponder

Emotions are contagious. Make sure yours are worth catching.

— Anonymous

Secret #3

Finishing Well
vs.
Finishing First:
Building Collaboration

When I was a young girl, my parents took me on a trip to northern California, where we visited the huge sequoia trees. I was really impressed and awed by the tree that was so big that my dad could drive our car through its trunk! Later I found out that those trees, which are the tallest trees in the world, actually have shallow root systems. So how do they stay upright? Many of them don't. Most fall to the ground and die. The ones that manage to stand tall in the forest are the ones with limbs that are balanced and roots that intertwine with the roots of the surrounding trees. By intertwining their roots, the trees help one another to live.

Later I found out that those trees, which are the tallest trees in the world, actually have shallow root systems. So how do they stay upright? Many of them don't. Most fall to the ground and die.

Those trees remind me of uncommon leaders. Uncommon leaders don't just try to get those they lead to be loyal to them. Uncommon leaders place a premium on collaboration. The goal is not just to finish first. Yes, you want high test scores and high achievement in your school. But you also want to maintain that positive atmosphere I talked about as part of secret number 2.

I would define "finishing well" as reaching your goals while maintaining emotional balance—and the best way I know to do that is through a positive, collaborative process. Uncommon leaders know the power of a group that is enthusiastic about its mission to help everyone succeed. The group morale becomes a valuable commodity in an environment like that, because collaborative efforts result in powerful connections among peers: everyone nurtures everyone else. This camaraderie has the potential to produce wonderful results.

Most of us would agree that a group of people working together can accomplish more than those same people working on their own. Michael Fullan talks about "helping all employees find meaning, increased skill development, and personal satisfaction in making contributions that *simultaneously* fulfill their own goals and the goals of the organization (the needs of the customers expressed in achievement terms)" (Fullan 2008, 25). Apply that theory to the school environment. Do you see what I mean? You can finish well *and* finish first!

A Side Benefit

When you develop a strong sense of community within your school, it can have another benefit, too. Sometimes a teacher will stay with a particular school even when he gets an offer of another job with a better salary. The psychological need that's being met in the current position—the need for a solid sense of community—can be that important.

I remember one year when the school where I was serving as principal had a significant bilingual population. Bilingual teachers were hard to come by, so a neighboring district offered a huge signing bonus to lure teachers from other districts. One of our bilingual teachers told me that she'd decided not to apply. She said she knew that she could make more money at the other school, but she couldn't leave the tight-knit team of teachers she was working with. She told me that because she felt so accepted by the other members of her team and so sure of their loyalty to her, she would never even consider leaving.

The Human Doings Approach

The goal in the Human Doings approach is finishing first at the expense of finishing well (together). At one point when I was a young teacher, I worked for a principal who used the Human Doings approach a lot. When you got a note in your box that he wanted to see you, it never meant anything good. It was sort of like getting sent to a detention hall for teachers. I always felt as if I should put on full-body armor when I went to see him. He never smiled or made eye contact during those meetings. He didn't talk much, but when he did, it was quick, to the point, and usually negative. It didn't help that I couldn't get support or encouragement from other teachers in those early years because I didn't know them; all we had in common was a parking lot. The only ones I knew were the ones who were in line with me at the "ditto" machine. (If you're old enough, you remember ditto machines. They came before photocopiers. They had purple ink that would get all over your clothes, and the kids loved smelling the freshly cranked sheets they produced.) There was a lot of competition in that school and not much collaboration.

We know more now about effective communication, but it can still be easy to fall into the habit of negative monitoring. You pore over a set of test data like a statistician. You look for weaknesses, are quick to point them out, and use punishment to direct behavior. You don't spend much energy on collegiality and cooperation or on balancing a focus on tasks with a focus on relationships. This can set up competition in an organization rather than collaboration. It is what has been called "stick power," or using intimidation or threats to change behavior. An example would be calling in a teacher and pointing out all the negatives—test scores, parent comments, whatever—without addressing effective actions she could take and without working to help that teacher improve. This becomes a negative form of micromanaging. The teacher is left thinking just about her classroom and not about the school as a whole. She's isolated and doesn't make meaningful connections with colleagues who might be able to help her.

Just one instance of treating someone in this Human Doings way can destroy the morale of the entire staff.

One of the things this approach fails to recognize is that everyone observes the way any one teacher is treated by the leader. Other teachers then decide whether the leader can be trusted based on that data. Just one instance of treating someone in this Human Doings way can destroy the morale of the entire staff, as each person assumes that he could be treated the same way. Someone who takes the Human Doings approach tends to see everyone as part of an assembly line, and ultimately that can make that assembly line break down.

The Human Beings Approach

This approach involves the purposeful connecting of teachers to one another, just like those sequoia trees, so that the school becomes a place where everyone cares about, looks after, and roots for everyone else. In this type of environment, teachers become part of something larger than themselves. They work together for the good of the whole. If the Human Doings approach is to punitively micromanage and police the place, the Human Beings approach is to provide direction and create conditions that encourage individual and collective commitment to doing outstanding work. Everyone is inspired, everyone grows, and the organization flourishes in the process. So instead of viewing others as part of an assembly line, the leader who takes the Human Beings approach sees others as brimming with possibilities and potential.

It's important to be clear about what I mean here. If you don't think of collaboration as a dynamic process, you might feel pressured to support everyone equally each and every day. That's not realistic, and I would suggest that it's not necessary. Instead, think about providing appropriate support so that, *over time*, everyone will reach her potential.

Let's say you have a teacher we'll call Anita. Anita is expecting a baby and is having a difficult pregnancy. Anita needs your support. For the time being, you may decide to take away some of her responsibilities, such as bus duty or recess duty, that would require her to be on her feet.

For now, Anita is the priority; the other teachers will have to wait their turn. If the group is functional, everyone will understand and finish well in the end.

You hear so much these days about the importance of collaboration in education. Lots of books are written about it. You read articles about it and go to workshops dealing with it, but in my opinion, one important piece of the puzzle has been missing from the discussion: Everyone needs support. However, not everyone has to get that support at the same time or in the same way.

Think about the students in your building. You want the teachers to differentiate their instruction. You don't want the "one size fits all" approach to teaching in the classroom. At the same time, you know that differentiating instruction means that fair is not always equal. Fair is the recognition by teachers that no two students are the same. Some learn quickly, and some do not. All learn in different ways. When teachers differentiate instruction, they give support on certain days and in appropriate ways to those students who need it. Over time, all the students do well. Differentiation means designing experiences for students that will enable each student to learn the curriculum well.

When you promote collaboration, you need to recognize once again that fair is not necessarily equal. In the end, however, everyone will finish well.

Thus, the third secret of inspiring your team is to foster collaboration. The uncommon leader makes it a point to connect teachers with one another in purposeful and positive ways, to affirm teachers as special people, and to help everyone to finish first (with high achievement) and to finish well (emotionally balanced).

Tips for Building Collaboration

Tune in to MMFG-AM

Someone once told me that everyone is always listening to a certain radio station. It's an AM station with the call letters MMFG-AM. That stands for "Make me feel good about me!" Psychologists call this the "affiliative need," which means that inside each of us is a need to belong.

Uncommon leaders keep this in mind. They plan activities and time for teachers to get to know one another on a personal level and to build relationships. Uncommon leaders know that this is not fluff, but crucial to the kind of trust that must exist if teachers are to collaborate positively and purposefully.

Get Away from It All

As a back-to-school ritual, plan a retreat for the staff at a location other than the school. When teachers have the opportunity to leave campus, they bond more than when they just have casual conversations at school. Creativity increases because teachers are not distracted by the usual routines.

Laugh Out Loud

Did you know that at SeaWorld parks, before the trainers begin to teach the animals the tricks they will do in the shows, the trainers first play with the animals? They get into the water and just play. Isn't that a great idea?

Laughter produces changes in heart rate, blood pressure, and respiration similar to those seen after strenuous exercise. Teachers don't get to laugh or have as much fun as they'd like. Find something that makes you and your teachers laugh together, and enjoy it regularly.

At our faculty meetings, we used to have what I called a "kid break." If a teacher had a funny story about something a student had said or done, she would share it with the rest of us. I've always believed that most people would rather be entertained than educated. If you can do both, people will be clamoring to be part of your team.

Form an Appreciation Circle

End each faculty meeting with an appreciation circle. Have teachers stand or sit in a circle and express appreciation to one another. For instance, one person might appreciate another for coming up with a great student activity or for working with a special student. We all want to feel appreciated, and this is one way to encourage expressions of appreciation.

Walk & Talk

Start a faculty meeting with the "3Q walk." Ask each teacher to find a partner from a different grade level or department, then have them go for just a five-minute walk outside, around the building. While they're walking, they must each answer three questions: What is the best thing that happened to you today? What is a promise you have made to yourself? What is your goal for tomorrow? The fresh air, exercise, and conversation with a colleague will help everyone return in a better mood for the meeting.

Tools for Building Collaboration

ONE & ALL

Purpose:

This is a great activity to help teachers learn about one another and find things they have in common. It can also help identify the unique gifts and talents each member brings to the group.

Materials:

For Each Group: Graphic organizer (based on illustration on next page); pen or pencil

Time:

10 minutes

Procedure:

1. Divide participants into groups of four.

2. Have each group appoint a leader/recorder. Give each leader a copy of the graphic organizer (or give instructions and have each leader draw the organizer on his own); make sure he has a pen or pencil.

3. Have each group brainstorm five things the members have in common. Ask the group leader to write the five items in the center of the circle. For example, teachers in one group might figure out that they're all parents, all love to read, and so on.

4. Have each person in the group find one thing that's unique about himself. This must be something that's true for that person but not for the other people in the group. For example, the group might include three women and one man. The unique thing about the man is that he's the only male in the group.

5. Ask each group leader to stand up and share with everyone the five items the group has in common.

6. Ask each person to share with everyone what makes him unique within his group.

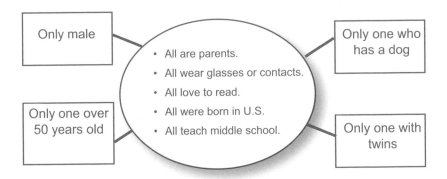

THE TOURNAMENT

Purpose:

> This activity is especially good for the beginning of the school year. It helps teachers think about their goals and focus on their common bond of helping all students succeed.

Materials:

> <u>For Each Teacher:</u> Graphic organizer (based on illustration); pen or pencil
>
> <u>For the Leader:</u> Chart paper; marker

Time:

> 10–20 minutes

Procedure:

> 1. Give each teacher a copy of the graphic organizer (or give instructions and have each person draw it on his own); make sure everyone has a pen or pencil.
>
> 2. Ask teachers to daydream for a few minutes about what they hope to accomplish with their students this year. Ask questions such as "What characteristics do you hope to develop?" and "What qualities do you want to see each student have?"

3. Ask each teacher to write down eight of her thoughts on the graphic organizer. Explain that each word or phrase should be written next to a number on the organizer.

4. Have each teacher choose one word or phrase from each "bracket" as the more important of the two.

5. Have each teacher continue narrowing down her choices until she comes up with the one word or phrase that she feels is the most important to her.

6. Ask each teacher to share her most important word or phrase with the group.

7. Write the "winning" words and phrases from the group on a large piece of chart paper for everyone to see. Talk about how similar the words and phrases are, and discuss things the teachers can do as a group to ensure these outcomes for the students.

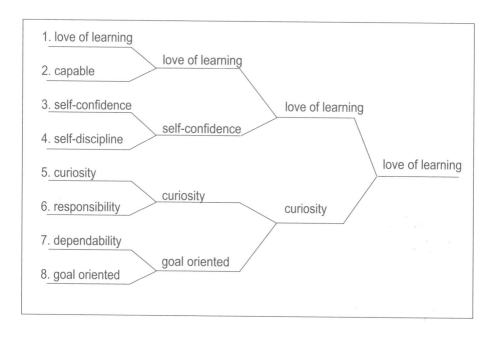

PIG PROFILES

Purpose:

This activity is a fun way to get teachers to learn about themselves and one another.

Materials:

For Each Teacher: Paper and pen or pencil

Time:

5–10 minutes

Procedure:

1. Give each teacher a sheet of paper and make sure each has a pen or pencil.

2. Ask each teacher to draw a pig on her piece of paper. Do not give any specific directions about the drawing; just say that each person should draw a pig.

3. After teachers have finished, explain what the pig drawings show about the people who created them. You might tell everyone to look at these specific attributes of their pigs:

    - *Position of the pig on the paper.* If the pig is at the top of the paper, the person is positive and optimistic. If it's in the middle of the paper, the person is a realist. If it's at the bottom, the person is a pessimist.

      - *Directionality.* If the drawing shows the pig head-on, the person is direct, likes to play the devil's advocate, and does not fear or avoid conflict. If the pig is facing to the right, the person is creative and innovative; is kind of spacey; and can't remember names, dates, or phone numbers. If the pig is facing to the left, the person doesn't have strong family ties and is pretty much a loner.

    - *Details.* If the drawing has many details, the person is analytical, cautious, and distrustful. If the drawing has

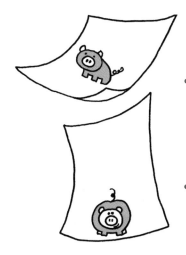

few details, the person is emotional, is a risk taker, and does not like projects with a lot of details.

- *Number of legs.* A pig with four legs means that the person is secure and sticks to his ideas. Fewer than four legs means that the person is insecure or going through a period of major change.

- *Size of ears.* The bigger the better! Big ears mean a good listener.

4. Give participants a chance to compare notes and learn about each other. At the same time, encourage them in discovering how all of their different attributes complement each other and contribute to the strength of the whole group.

TEAM POSTERS

Purpose:

This activity helps groups to bond and to set norms (working agreements) regarding how members will work together to complete a project.

Materials:

For Each Group: Chart paper; colored markers; sticky notes

Time:

10–20 minutes

Procedure:

1. Give each group a piece of chart paper, markers, and sticky notes. Describe and ask them to draw a graphic organizer like the one in the illustration.

2. Ask each group to come up with a team name and write it in the top left-hand box.

3. Ask each group to create a sign or symbol for their team and write it in the top right-hand box.

4. Ask each group to come up with a slogan or motto and write it in the bottom left-hand box.

5. Have each group member write something on a sticky note that she will agree to do in order to make the group's time together as powerful as possible. For example, someone might agree to listen with an open mind to the opinions of other team members. Tell the members to post their sticky notes in the bottom right-hand box of the poster.

6. If several groups are involved, you might want to ask the groups to share their posters.

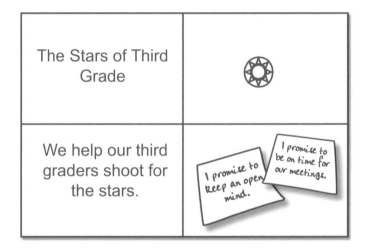

TWO TRUTHS & A LIE

Purpose:

> This activity is great for getting acquainted.

Materials:

> <u>For Each Teacher:</u> Paper and pen or pencil

Time:

> 10–20 minutes

Procedure:

1. Give each teacher a sheet of paper and make sure each has a pen or pencil.

2. Ask teachers how many of them have ever told a lie. Tell them that those with their hands down can now raise them, because that is definitely a lie!

3. Ask them to think of two things that are true about them and one thing that is a lie—but a believable lie.

4. Ask each teacher to write down his two truths and one lie.

5. Give teachers several minutes to let others read their three statements and to guess which of the three is the lie. If one person is not able to correctly guess another person's lie, have the person who can't guess sign the other person's paper.

6. When you call time, ask teachers to return to their seats and count their signatures. Find out who has the most signatures and declare that person the winner. Caution teachers to be careful, because this person is the best liar on the staff!

Liar! Liar!

Before teachers start writing their truths and lies, you might want to model the activity by giving them two truths and a lie about yourself. Let them guess which one is the lie.

SQUARE, CIRCLE, TRIANGLE, SQUIGGLE

Purpose:

> Like the pig activity, this one is guaranteed to get teachers laughing as they learn about themselves and one another in a fun way.

Materials:

> <u>For Each Person:</u> Paper and pen or pencil

Time:

> 5–10 minutes

Procedure:

1. Give each teacher a sheet of paper and make sure each has a pen or pencil.

2. Ask each teacher to draw the following four shapes: square, circle, triangle, and squiggly line.

3. Ask each teacher to pick the one shape that feels the most like him at the moment and put an X on it. Tell them not to think too hard; each person should just follow his first impulse.

4. Ask those who marked the square to stand up while you talk about them. Tell teachers that "squares" are highly organized; they like to make lists and then check things off as those things are accomplished. Say that they have great filing systems, with all the files labeled so that they know where everything is. Then explain that the drawback with squares is that they're resistant to change.

5. Have the squares sit down and ask those who marked the triangle to stand up. Tell teachers that "triangles" are the leaders. Triangles always want to know the bottom line, and they hate little games like this one! The drawback with triangles is that they can be a little bit bossy.

6. Have the triangles sit down and ask the "circles" to stand up. There will probably be a lot of these in the group. Acknowledge that and tell them that's always the case, because circles are the nicest people in the world—and

certainly teachers are! Circles are positive and always have a smile on their faces. The drawback with circles is that they just might get an ulcer one day by trying to keep everyone else happy.

7. Have the circles sit down and ask those who marked the squiggly line to stand up. Ask, "Have you ever heard the expression 'The lights are on, but nobody is home'?" These are the "squiggles"—creative and fun loving. The drawback with squiggles is this: Look at their desks. There are piles everywhere, but they don't want you to touch anything, because they know where everything is and they don't want you to mess things up!

8. Tell teachers to pretend that you've called a faculty meeting. The squares hope to get the meeting agenda in their boxes during the day so that they can bring it to the meeting and check off things that are done. The triangles go to the meeting because they have to, but they sit in the back with their arms folded and think, "It doesn't matter what anyone says. I'm going to go back to my classroom, close the door, and do what I've always done." The circles get to the meeting early—not because of the meeting itself, but because of the food and the socializing! The squiggles don't even know that there *is* a meeting, but they're smart: they've made friends with a square or a triangle, and they know that person will get them there.

9. Tell teachers that everyone is at the meeting. The squiggles have all the creative ideas; the squares don't want to change to incorporate these ideas; the triangles don't think they'll ever have the resources or the time to do what's been proposed; and the circles just want everyone to calm down!

10. Finally, you get to make your point: we're all different, but we all have something to contribute to the team.

BRIDGE BUILDING

Purpose:

> This activity encourages teachers to collaborate and to share plans, information, and resources. It also promotes a friendly and cooperative climate.

Materials:

> Shared by Everyone: Empty box about the size of a photocopier paper box; lady's purse containing a fair number of items; chart tablet and marker (optional).
>
> For Each Group: Roll of 1/2-inch masking tape; 12- to 14-inch stack of old newspapers

Time:

> 30–45 minutes

Procedure:

1. Place the box and the purse at the front of the room.

2. Form groups of approximately eight teachers. Hand out the masking tape and newspapers.

3. Explain that each group is going to build a bridge high enough so that the box can pass under it and strong enough to support the purse. Tell teachers that the newspapers can be taped only to the floor, not to a wall or a person.

4. Ask each group to select one person to look at both the box and the purse. The person is allowed to pick up the purse to get a sense of its weight.

5. Give each group seven minutes of planning time. When the planning time is up, hide the box and the purse.

6. Give the groups 10 minutes of building time. When the building time is up, pass the purse and the box around so that each group can test its bridge.

7. Ask group members to sit around their bridges.

Processing This Activity

Ask questions that have to do with leadership; decision making; and roles, tasks, and responsibilities. Just pick a category, toss out questions (see the box for ideas), and give the groups a few minutes to discuss them. Ask each group to share its discussion with the whole group. Acknowledge that participants will probably not be called on to build a paper bridge, but ask what they learned about planning and working with a group—things that might help any group work together better. They might say that it's important to get everyone's ideas, to use their planning time well, and so on.

Sample Questions for Bridge Builders

Leadership

- Who were the leaders?
- Did the leadership role shift?
- Did everybody have a turn?
- How did the leaders get acknowledged?
- What did the leaders do that helped the group?

Decision Making

- How did you share ideas?
- How did your group make decisions?
- Did the loudest get what she wanted?
- Did the plans change?

Roles, Tasks & Responsibilities

- Did you utilize people's individual skills?
- How did you determine what you would do?
- What were the different roles?
- How do you think you worked as a group?

JUST LIKE ME

Purpose:

> This activity helps teachers get to know one another as they build rapport.

Materials:

> <u>For Each Teacher:</u> M&M's (or substitute jelly beans or other counters)

Time:

> 10–20 minutes

Procedure:

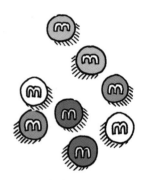

1. If the whole group has more than 10 people, divide participants into groups of four or five.

2. Pass out the M&M's, giving the same number to each person.

3. Have each person take a turn naming something she's done that others in the group may or may not have done.

4. Tell anyone in the group who has done the same thing to put an M&M in the middle of the table.

5. Declare the person who runs out of candy first to be the "most experienced!"

I HAVE A DREAM

Purpose:

> This activity focuses teachers on the common goals of teaching and learning. It also points out that the ways the group collaborates will affect its success in meeting its goals.

Materials:

> 5- to 6-inch pieces of yarn in several different colors (1 piece per person)

Time:

10–20 minutes

Procedure:

1. Ask each teacher to select a piece of yarn for the activity and to think of a "dream" for the school.

2. Have each teacher find someone in the room who's holding a different-colored piece of yarn. Tell the pair to share their dreams with each other and tie their pieces of yarn together.

3. Now ask each pair to find another pair with more strips of yarn with whom they can share their dreams. Have them tie that pair's yarn onto theirs while discussing all dreams.

4. Repeat until all the pieces of yarn are tied together and a circle of yarn has been formed.

5. Ask teachers to talk about the ways in which our dreams can bind us together.

IF I COULD . . .

Purpose:

This is a great get-acquainted activity.

Materials:

None

Time:

10–20 minutes

Procedure:

1. Have small groups of teachers sit in a circle.

2. Have teachers take turns responding to prompts such as:

   • If I could, I would learn to . . .

   • If I could, I would like to meet . . .

   • If I could, I would travel to . . .

- If I could, I would spend more time . . .
- If I could, I would always . . .
- If I could, I would never . . .
- If I could, I would change . . .

TOILET PAPER TALES

Purpose:

This is another fun way for teachers to get to know one another. Use it with discretion, though. Revealing this much personal information makes some folks uncomfortable!

Materials:

Several rolls of toilet paper

Time:

10–20 minutes

Procedure:

1. Tell teachers that there is a shortage of toilet paper for the day, so each person will need to tear off the number of sheets he thinks he will need. (Keep a straight face. They will believe you.)

2. Pass around the rolls of toilet paper so that each teacher can tear off what he thinks he'll need.

3. After each person has torn off his portion, tell everyone to count the number of sheets he's holding.

4. Have each person stand up and tell the group one thing about himself for each sheet of paper he tore off the roll.

M&M'S

Purpose:

This activity helps teachers get to know one another. Only when there is a trusting environment can teachers speak openly and consider the diverse opinions of others.

Materials:

For Each Teacher: Mini-package of M&M's

Shared by Everyone: Chart with cues related to the colors of the M&M's (see box for examples)

Time:

10–20 minutes

Procedure:

1. Have participants form groups of four to six.
2. Give each teacher a package of M&M's.
3. Ask teachers to open their packages and spread the M&M's out in front of them.
4. Have them take turns choosing one of their M&M's and responding to the cues on the chart.

Sample M&M's Cues

Green: I am most talented when . . .

Red: I am the best teacher when . . .

Yellow: I like myself best when . . .

Blue: I am most likely to succeed when . . .

Orange: I am best-looking when . . .

Brown: I am most friendly when . . .

A Pearl to Ponder

Never doubt that a small group of thoughtful, committed people can change the world. Indeed, it is the only thing that ever has.

—Margaret Mead

Secret #4

Shift Happens:
Facilitating Change

Remember the summer when I was so excited about opening that new school? Remember the story I told you about Nancy and the green cabinet? Well, you need to understand that only a few months before that, I had actually been questioning my decision to accept the position at that school.

You must be thinking, "This woman is crazy! Didn't she just say that she was super excited about that opportunity? Didn't she say she was on cloud nine?" Well, yes. That's true. When I applied, I did really want the professional opportunity that I believed opening a new school could afford. I anxiously awaited the call from the district office letting me know whether I had been selected as principal. And then, on the Friday before spring break, I finally got the call.

I'll never forget my initial reaction. I was running around my house shouting, "I can't believe they picked me!

I'm so excited!" But by Monday, I wasn't feeling so elated. In fact, I was starting to question my decision to accept the position—and my husband and children were completely baffled by my behavior. I was saying things like "Why did I do this? I feel so comfortable in the school where I am now. I know all the teachers, the parents, the students, the community. What have I done? What if I can't do this? What if . . .? What if . . .? What if . . .?"

Then, just when I was thinking I was going to have to take tranquilizers to get through the whole thing, I had an idea. I called another principal, Becky, who lived in my neighborhood and who had opened two schools herself. I asked her if I could come over and pick her brain. As we sat by her pool sipping our favorite beverages, she gave me some great advice. In fact, I spent most of spring break at her house sipping and talking, sipping and talking, and eventually getting the courage I needed to forge ahead. So instead of calling the district and telling them I had changed my mind—something I had considered seriously that first weekend—I began the work of opening that new school.

What was going on? And what was it that made the differ-ence and gave me the courage to go ahead?

Looking back now, I realize that deciding to take that job was one of the best professional decisions I've ever made. But what in the world happened to me in those early days of a dream coming true? I almost didn't even take the position! And in the end, what it all came down to was that I was really scared of the change I was about to make. What was going on? And what was it that made the difference and gave me the courage to go ahead?

What made the difference for me was Becky. For one thing, my friend helped me understand the technical aspects of the change I was facing—the "stuff" that needed to be done to open the new building. You probably know about the "implementation dip" that everyone who is trying something new goes through. Your teachers go through that dip when they begin anything new in their classrooms—whether it is differentiating instruction or implementing a new reading program. Things always get worse before they get better. I knew I'd be facing what I call the "practical dip," and that was part of what had me so overwhelmed.

But I was dealing with more than just technical issues. I was feeling fear, sadness, and outright terror. You see, the other part of the change process is the emotional part—the Human Beings part. I call this the "psychological dip." Whenever you're faced with making a change—whether you perceive the change as good or bad—you go through certain normal and predictable emotional stages.

Let me give you an example. Let's say that you find out you're going to have a baby. Let's also say that you're excited about this change. The first stage of the change process is denial. You may say something like "Wow! I'm thrilled. We're expecting a baby! I just can't believe it! We've waited so long!" But when you bring the baby home, you experience the next stage, "the dip." That includes both the "practical dip," as you learn how to change diapers, bathe the baby, and so on, and the "psychological dip."

The normal stages of the psychological dip include anger, depression, sadness, fear, and so on. You might be thinking, "What if I drop the baby?" or "I miss a good night's sleep" or "I want my freedom to come and go as I please!" And remember, this was a change you were excited about! As you adjust to your new role and integrate this new person into your life, you eventually come to the last stage of the process, acceptance. So whether you're excited or not excited about a change, you usually can't avoid the three stages that come with it: denial, "the dip," and acceptance (Menninger, 1988).

Let's look at an example that's closer to the world of education. Have you ever had the experience of getting to leave your school and attend a professional development conference for a few days at the district's expense? If so, that was a change in your routine—probably a change you were excited about. I bet that when you found out you were going, you probably said something like "Wow! This is a great opportunity for me! I can't believe I was chosen to go!" That was a classic first-stage comment—denial.

If you have a significant other at home, do not go home and tell that person what a wonderful time you had.

Then you went to the conference—still sky-high over this chance to get away for a few days. Well, I don't know exactly when, but sometime after you arrived, checked into your hotel, and so on, you probably started thinking something like, "I wonder what's going on at school? Maybe I should call." Then maybe you started thinking, "I wish I could sleep in my own bed. I don't sleep well in hotel rooms." These are classic symptoms of "the dip."

Finally, you got in the swing of being away, eating out, and so on. You'd entered the acceptance stage—and if you're like me, you probably hit that stage just about the time you had to go home. (One hint: If you have a significant other at home, do not go home and tell that person what a wonderful time you had. If asked, just say, "It was okay." I did learn that the hard way!)

When I learned that I'd been selected for that new job, the comment I repeatedly annoyed my family with—"I just can't believe they picked me!"—reflected the first stage, denial. Then I experienced the practical dip as I worried about how to hire staff, order materials for the new building, and so on. I also experienced the psychological dip as I started to feel both sad and fearful. I was annoying everyone at my house even more during that stage by telling them I was going to reconsider my decision.

Then along came my peer and friend, Becky, who took me under her wing and helped me get through these dips— both the practical dip and the psychological one. She gave me plenty of practical advice about the "stuff" of opening a new school, but she also paid attention to the emotions I was feeling. She reassured me that my feelings were normal and that I would get through them and go on to truly enjoy the exciting challenges ahead. She was the uncommon leader I needed during that time; she facilitated my progress in getting to the acceptance stage and building my confidence that I could handle what was ahead of me. Everybody needs a Becky!

The Human Doings Approach

The Human Doings approach to facilitating change deals only with the technical aspects and the accompanying dip in performance as people begin to implement the change. Many times what happens is that in your desire to do the best for your students, you end up introducing a bunch of changes that can leave a staff exhausted. In this approach, the leader sees each change as an "event," integrates the changes himself, and expects continued integration of the changes by the staff on a rapid timetable. He doesn't realize that change is a process and that he must also address the Human Beings side of the process.

In your desire to do the best for your students, you end up introducing a bunch of changes that can leave a staff exhausted.

I certainly operated like this the first year I was a principal. I'm sure that some people thought my goal that year was to be the "innovation queen." I would sign the staff up for any innovations that came my way. On any given day, we could be working with peer coaching, learning styles, multiple intelligences, quality teams, whole language, cooperative learning, mastery learning, and more. I was becoming the "fad facilitator," not the "learning facilitator." I couldn't understand why the teachers were not as excited and committed to all of my ideas as I was. Then one day a teacher told me that she just couldn't keep up with it all. She said that she wasn't burned-out yet, but she was "a little crisp"!

The Human Beings Approach

Uncommon leadership calls for understanding and appreciating the dips of the change process—both the practical dip and the psychological dip. As I got more years of being a principal under my belt, I became more sensitive to the human side of change. I remember a time, for example, when I was working with a difficult teacher. You know the type—she retired and just forgot to tell anybody. To meet the needs of her students, who were becoming more diverse every year, she needed to introduce more flexible grouping in her classroom. I sent her to some workshops to learn ways to group flexibly. Then one day I decided to stop by her room to see what was going on. I was so pleased to find her students in small groups. However, a second look told me a different story. The teacher was still stuck in the old position: sitting at the overhead projector in front of the class, just talking at them. She hadn't changed her teaching approach. She just had the students sitting in small groups!

A few years earlier, I probably would have reacted in the Human Doings way, thinking only that this teacher was driving me nuts and was incredibly resistant to change. However, this time I chose the Human Beings way. I considered that although this teacher could be resisting change, she could also be very scared. I needed to be sensitive to the reality that every change is a mess in the middle. I needed to support the technical aspects of the change to more flexible groups, but I also needed to support the human side of the change process. Understanding that side of the process helped lessen the anger I might have felt toward this teacher and allowed me to support her emotional journey through the changes I was asking her to make. By acknowledging her feelings and explaining to her that those feelings were a normal part of the process, I helped her integrate this new way of teaching into her routine.

And that brings us to the fourth secret of inspiring those you lead: supporting the Human Beings side of the change process.

Tips for Facilitating Change

Make the Vision Yours—and Only Yours

Without a vision, change will be difficult. You can have a great campus improvement plan and lots of innovations and programs in place, but without a clear and compelling statement of where you're heading, those change efforts won't get very far. In fact, instead of lasting change, you might end up with lasting confusion. You've probably been told to make sure you and those you lead collaborate to develop the vision. I'm going to suggest a slightly different approach. My suggestion is for you to develop your vision alone, because only you know what your passion is for your school. (You'll still involve the rest of the staff, of course. I'll come back to that in a minute.)

It's not hard to do this. When I opened the new school, I was totally alone in terms of developing a vision for that school. So I really thought about what I wanted to guarantee every student and staff member who walked in the door each day. In about two or three sentences, I nailed it. Then what? Once that vision was clear, I had the most important information I needed to make many of the important decisions involved in opening a new school. I'm not talking about where to hang the clocks in each classroom. I'm talking about the decisions that affect students. All I had to do was weigh my answer against the vision I had created. Would hiring this teacher further the vision? Would ordering these materials support the vision? Should I use this personnel allocation for a teacher or a literacy coach? The list went on and on.

Once that vision was clear, I had the most important information I needed to make many of the important decisions involved in opening a new school.

Get Their Buy-In in a Creative Way

Once I had my vision and had hired the staff, I decided to have a one-day off-site retreat before the school year started. I felt it was important to meet away from the new school before the school year started. (See secret number 3 for more about the power of off-site meetings.) I wanted a day with the staff without any interruptions—not only to start building the relationships I knew were so crucial but also to start building the buy-in to my vision.

During the retreat, I talked to the group as a whole about my vision. They had all heard it many times during the interview process, but today I wanted them to think about what it meant to them. We tried a simple and fun activity based on the vision. I divided the staff into grade-level groups and asked each group to come up with one way to show the vision in action. Some grade levels put on skits; some wrote and performed songs; some drew posters. But by the end of the time allotted, each group had massaged that vision. They were starting to make it their own.

Communicate That Vision

It's not enough to spend time and energy creating your vision and getting others to buy into it. You know that. The vision also has to be communicated. That means more than just hanging it on the wall, printing it at the top of the campus improvement plans or weekly newsletter, or displaying it on the marquee in front of the school. That's not enough. It's also not enough to make speeches about it to the various stakeholders. The vision has to become part of the culture; it has to become "the way we do things around here." You are key to accomplishing that. Hour by hour, minute by minute, you have to walk the walk and incorporate messages about the vision into your activities. Your behavior can never ever undermine the vision.

I'm sure you have a vision; most schools do now. And I bet you are really good at being *aware* of your vision. But given the day-to-day pressures of being a principal, it's easy to forget to *communicate* the vision. Don't let that happen. Make the following question number one on your daily "to do" list: "How can I communicate the vision today?" And think about this question: "Would the teachers, if asked today, be able to articulate the vision to others?" Then think about your day, and no matter what it entails—a meeting, an observation in a classroom, reading a story to students— think about how you can use each task to further the vision. It's very difficult to facilitate change if people don't have a firm understanding of where they are headed. Truly understanding and incorporating the vision into their own thinking will help teachers know where to focus their efforts each day.

Give Feedback That Feeds

One of the best by-products of having a vision is the guidance it gives you in providing feedback to others, especially when you're trying to implement change. When you have to give corrective feedback to someone, frame it in terms of whether the vision is being furthered. Your feedback will feed the vision. There is so much power in saying to a teacher or even to a parent (as I have done), "Your behavior is not aligned with the vision for our school." Whoa! The person can disagree with you, but he can't question your motives. If you're asking a teacher to change, for example, you can enhance that teacher's capacity for change by making it clear that the change supports the vision.

Remember That Patience Is a Virtue

I can be a very impatient person. If I want something, I tend to want it now. This can be a good thing, but when it comes to dealing with change, it can also be a not-so-good thing. Remember how, as part of secret number 2, we talked about being a "finder"—trying to catch someone doing something well? Being a finder is especially important when it comes to implementing change. Look for instances, baby steps even, in which others are living out the vision. If you look, you will find them. When you find them, be all over them.

For example, let's say your vision includes maximizing the growth of each student. One day during an informal

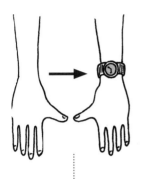

walk-through, you notice a regular-education teacher really helping an inclusion student. Put your watch on your other hand (that's what I do to remember something important), and as soon as you get back to your office, write that teacher a quick note letting her know exactly what you saw that supported the school's vision.

In Michael Fullan's *The Six Secrets of Change*, he cautions new leaders in particular when he writes, "Don't roll your eyes on one day when you see practice that is less than effective by your standards. Instead, invest in capacity building while suspending short-term judgment" (Fullan 2008, 58). Celebrate those small successes!

Tools for Facilitating Change

BELIEF STATEMENTS

Purpose:

This activity helps get teachers involved in shaping the vision.

Materials:

Chart paper; markers; colored dots

Time:

20–30 minutes

Procedure:

1. Come up with about 20 "belief statements"—things you think it will take to make your vision become a reality. See the box for examples.

2. Write the belief statements on chart paper and hang the chart paper around the room.

3. Encourage the group to read and discuss the statements.

4. Give each teacher three or four colored dots (color doesn't matter).

5. Ask teachers to use their dots to "vote" for the belief statements they agree with most strongly. A teacher can use all of his dots to mark one belief statement, or he can mark several different statements.

6. The voting provides a visual of which belief statements the staff feels most passionate about. Follow up with a discussion of why teachers feel especially strongly about those statements.

For Example

You might head your chart with a statement such as "I believe that making our vision a reality will require . . ." Then the list might include possibilities such as these:

- Differentiated instruction
- Ongoing assessment
- Nurturing the whole child
- Parents and partners

BACK-TO-BACK

Purpose:

> This activity is designed to help people understand that change is difficult and that most people don't like it. I have used it at faculty meetings and in workshops. It's fun, and it gets the point across!

Materials:

> None

Time:

> 5–10 minutes

Procedure:

1. Ask teachers to stand up. Have each one find a partner.

2. Tell the partners that the next 30 seconds will be the longest 30 seconds of their lives, because they are going to be looking each other over from head to toe without saying a word for that entire time. (You will likely get some chuckles here.)

3. Time the partners for 30 seconds.

4. Ask the teachers to turn back-to-back.

5. Explain that each person is to change three things about her appearance. For example, someone might move her watch to another wrist, take off her glasses, or remove an earring. Give the partners a few minutes to do this.

6. Ask the partners to check with each other. When both

are ready, have them turn around and take turns guessing what the other person changed.

7. After a few minutes, ask teachers to shake hands, thank their partners, and sit down.

Processing This Activity

Point out to participants what you noticed as you watched them: as soon as someone guessed what a partner had changed, the partner couldn't wait to get things back to "normal." (I've seen this happen every time.) The watch went back on the wrist; the glasses went back on the face. That is because change is uncomfortable for pretty much everyone. The only person who really likes change is a baby with a wet diaper!

STAGES OF CHANGE

Purpose:

This activity helps participants understand that all change involves predictable stages and that the process of dealing with change, whether it's perceived as a good change or a bad change, mirrors the process of coping with loss.

Materials:

For Each Group: Pen and paper

For the Leader: Chart tablet; markers

Time:

20–30 minutes

Procedure:

1. Ask participants to sit in groups of four or five.

2. Ask each participant to think of a change that he has experienced but that he did not ask for. Give examples such as a divorce, changing grade levels, or having a child move back home.

3. Ask each participant to remember the feelings he experienced, in chronological order, as he went through that change.

4. After about five minutes of individual reflection, ask each group to appoint a leader to begin a discussion. Explain that individuals don't have to identify the specific changes they're thinking of, but they do need to share the feelings they experienced, in the order in which they experienced them. Instruct the groups to listen for similarities in both the feelings individuals express and the order of those feelings. Ask someone in each group to record the feelings each individual describes. Make sure the recorder has pen and paper.

5. After about 15 minutes, tell the participants to thank one another.

Processing This Activity

Ask the whole group if they heard similar feelings and in a similar order from all the participants. They'll probably tell you that they did. Ask the groups to tell you the feelings individuals experienced. As they do, write them on the chart tablet for all to see.

Talk with the whole group about the psychological dips that occur with any innovation or change. Make sure they understand that all change, whether perceived as good or bad, will involve similar feelings. Remind them that dealing with change is a lot like dealing with loss. They need to understand that their feelings are normal and that they will be supported during the emotional journey that change involves. Challenge them not only to look to you for support but also to support one another during the various emotional stages of dealing with change.

Here's What Can Happen

I once used this activity with a staff when we were in the process of adopting a change at the district level that would affect all the campuses. It was a major change that would call for a reorganization of the curriculum. I knew that some teachers were excited about it, but most dreaded it. They just did not want to give up that dinosaur unit they had taught for the past 20 years! I felt that they needed to be aware of the process of change—both the practical and the human aspects. They needed to know that the feelings they would experience were normal and that they would have support.

At the end of the meeting, a really neat thing happened. The kindergarten teachers told me that they really liked the activity and planned to try it with the parents of their incoming students in the fall. They thought it would be a perfect way to illustrate to parents that having a child (especially the first one) start school is a major change and that the parents would experience similar feelings. The kindergarten teachers wanted the parents to understand that these feelings were normal and that the teachers would be there to support them.

This was one of those defining moments when I thought maybe something had really caught on. I decided to go back to my office, close my door, put my feet up, and just savor the moment. You know what happened then. Sure you do, because you've been there. As I was on the way back to my office, the secretary stopped me to say there was an angry parent on the phone. And that's the subject of the next chapter.

A Pearl to Ponder

Every new adjustment is a crisis in self-esteem.

—Eric Hoffer

Secret #5

Dangerous Opportunities:
Managing Conflict

When my daughter was in high school, she began dating a boy who attended a high school in a different community. She invited him to our home for dinner one evening so that her dad and I could meet him. Before the boy arrived, my husband was asking my daughter questions about him, hoping to find some things to talk about. In the course of the conversation, my daughter told her dad that the boy played football. "Great!" my husband thought. "Now there's something I can visit with him about." So the next question to my daughter was "What position does he play?" She thought a minute and said, "I'm not sure. I think he may be the drawback!"

The drawback! We got a good laugh out of that comment. Think about it, though. Why isn't there a position in football called the drawback? Probably because no one would want to be the drawback in a game. Isn't that how we feel about conflict? Conflict is generally perceived as negative. That's a problem, because leaders deal with conflict all the time.

In my early years as a principal, I really struggled with all the adult conflict that came to me. When I was an assistant principal, most of the conflict I dealt with was among students. I didn't have too much difficulty managing the conflict among the little people. But when I became a principal, the conflict among the big people drove me nuts. In fact, during my first year, I struggled so much with issues that involved solving conflict among teachers and parents that I decided I was going to have to either learn better ways to manage it all or find another job.

Dealing with conflict is certainly an inevitable part of leadership.

For a while, the option of finding another job was really appealing. I couldn't figure out why I was able to be contagiously enthusiastic most of the time but totally unable to cope when I was faced with conflict. So I signed up for every single workshop I could find that had anything to do with conflict resolution. I went; I learned; I studied; I tried to apply everything I was taught. So now, based on this often difficult journey of learning to deal with conflict, I hope that I can give you some advice for your journey. And that's important, because dealing with conflict is certainly an inevitable part of leadership.

One of the first things I learned was that conflict is not necessarily a bad thing at all. It's really what you do with conflict that counts. And that's the fifth secret of building a successful team. In my case, part of learning what to do with conflict was learning more about myself. I needed to know more about my own beliefs and attitudes so that I could handle conflict better. I also learned that conflict increases in a building where people are trying to make changes and that I needed to allow for the inevitable stormy stage of group development.

The Human Doings Approach

One way to avoid conflict is to surround yourself with weak people and keep tight control of everything. But who would want to do that? If you were surrounded by a bunch of yes-people, you'd eliminate conflict, but you'd also miss out on the joy that comes with helping others to grow and develop their own thinking. In my opinion, that's too much of a sacrifice.

Another Human Doings approach might be to avoid conflict by trying to please everyone. That was me during my first year as a principal. That approach wore me out both physically and emotionally, because I was dealing with too many people—the parents, the teachers, and the students—to be able to please all of them all the time.

A third approach might be to get into the habit of saying, "I don't want to hear about the issues you're having. Just work it out." A leader can't avoid all conflict by simply removing herself from it. Sometimes as principals we're so busy with the day-to-day tasks of the job that we send others a message we may not intend. The message we send others is, "Don't come to me unless it's really important." That kind of avoidance only creates more conflict.

The Human Beings Approach

The Human Beings approach recognizes that conflict is not necessarily bad and that sometimes the best decisions are made as a result of conflict. The Human Beings leader knows that hiring the best teachers available often increases conflict. The best teachers are usually independent and creative and completely devoted to their students. That means conflict! But hiring such teachers also brings different perspectives and wisdom to the table. The Human Beings leader understands that. He knows there will be conflict among his outstanding staff, and he lets teachers know that he will be available to help them resolve it. He makes it clear that they should let him know as soon as possible about a potential conflict so that the problem doesn't escalate.

The best teachers are usually independent and creative and completely devoted to their students. That means conflict!

The Human Beings leader also uses another strategy to handle conflict in a positive way: assume the best about those you lead, because then they will do everything they can to live up to your expectations. This leader knows that you really can bring out the productive and rational sides of just about anyone, even those "resident Nazis" in your building.

Tips for Managing Conflict

Don't Haggle

I used to feel that every conflict I was involved in ended up with the other person and me just haggling over our positions. Whether I was dealing with a parent who was demanding that I put her child in a certain teacher's classroom or the PTO president who wanted funds spent his way, it seemed that I often ended up haggling. Then I discovered something called "principled negotiation," a great tool from a little book titled *Getting to Yes* by Roger Fisher, William Ury, and Bruce Patton.

Basically, the process is designed to preserve relationships by creating agreements that satisfy the interests of both parties. It allows you to obtain what you want but still be decent to and respectful of others. It's an alternative to giving in, which can often leave you feeling bitter and exploited, or to taking a competitive stance, which can destroy the relationship. Instead, principled negotiation asks you to view the other person as your partner and to think of the process as trying to find a way to meet the interests of both parties. The process has four basic parts:

- Separate the people from the problem.

- Focus on interests and not positions.

- Generate a variety of options that are satisfying to both parties.

- Base the agreement on objective criteria.

What initially appealed to me about this approach was that it involves reframing the conflict to shift the focus from the person to the problem. I decided to try to use it as much as I could, because so much of the time at school, we want a "win-win" solution: we want an outcome that resolves the issue but leaves both parties feeling satisfied and still friendly. This approach did that, and it helped me a lot.

Let me give you an example. On the morning after the second graders' music program one May, the secretary greeted me as soon as I walked in the building. She told me that she had a very upset and angry parent on the phone. The caller was the mother of one of our second graders. When I took the call, I was stunned to find a mom crying uncontrollably on the other end of the phone. She told me that she was extremely upset over something to do with the second-grade program and that her husband was going to delay going in to work because they needed to talk with me right away. I told them to come in to school and I would see them.

One of the reasons I told them to come on in was that I wanted the music teacher included in the conference, and I knew that her planning period was the first period of the day. Well, she about freaked out when I told her these parents were coming in. She couldn't imagine what they were so upset about, and, of course, she thought that it must be something she'd done. I told her not to worry and that I would act as facilitator. I just wanted her there in case the issue did concern her. (Remember my norm of not talking about others behind their backs unless the talk can be positive.) I had a feeling that there was more to the problem than just the music program, however.

When the parents arrived, they told us they were very upset because their daughter had not had a speaking part in the program. Yes, you read that right. The husband had taken time off from work and the mother was bordering on hysteria all because their daughter had not had a speaking part in the second-grade program. The music teacher tried to explain to the parents that every student had been given the opportunity to say whether he or she wanted to try out for a speaking part and that their daughter had not expressed any interest in that at all.

Now, let's take a look at that situation and apply the process called principled negotiation. Right now we're at the positional level. Their position was "Our daughter must have a speaking part in your musicals." Our position was "No, we can't always guarantee such a thing." Can you imagine the haggling that could have taken place on this issue? And can you imagine how likely it was that no one would leave happy?

So what should I do? First, I needed to find out the interests of both parties. I certainly knew ours. If we'd given every student a speaking part, we would probably still be at the program, because at that time we had well over 160 second graders. But what were the parents' real interests?

I was fairly sure I knew what their interests were, because I had worked with them on several occasions during the year around issues with their daughter. She had some trouble adjusting and could be very withdrawn. As she would be entering that all-important third-grade year in the fall, I thought the parents were worried that she would fade into the woodwork, and they'd seized on the whole speaking part thing, turning that into the focus of the problem.

So guess what? I did that reframing I had learned about in principled negotiation. I got off the positions, and I said to the parents, "How can we make sure that next year, Mary [not her real name, of course] flourishes in third grade and also that when it comes time for the music program, she may or may not have a speaking part?"

Aha! I had changed the game. Now we were all problem solvers. Together we brainstormed some options, such as carefully placing her the next year. Everybody left happy, though the music teacher said no way would she ever want to be a principal!

Recognize Your Own Style

One of the things I had to do early on was examine my own relationship to conflict. All the workshops and strategies in the world wouldn't help me unless I could understand more about myself, how I viewed conflict, and why I saw it the way I did. In the process of developing that understanding, I found a book titled *Managing Conflict from the Inside Out,* by Marc Robert. It explains five styles of conflict management:

- *Competitive.* You see conflict only as win-lose, and all you're interested in is getting what you want.

- *Accommodating.* You're willing to let your own needs and interests go unmet in order to meet the needs and interests of the other person and maintain the relationship.

- *Avoiding.* You withdraw and don't even deal with the conflict.

- *Compromising.* You focus on each person giving up something.

- *Collaborative.* You actively work for a solution to the conflict that satisfies the needs and interests of both parties.

Certainly, some of these styles sound more appealing than others, but I learned that each one has a place in my tool kit for dealing with conflict. I also learned that each of us has a preferred style and that it's usually based on the style that our parents modeled for us. Well, that was a revelation for me! My mother was definitely the one in my family who dealt the most with conflict, and her style was accommodating. She tried to keep the peace with everyone. So naturally, when a major conflict erupted between parents and teachers the first year I was a principal, what style did I use? Yep, you got it—the accommodating one. I tried to make everyone happy. It was a natural instinct on my part, but it wasn't the right style for that problem.

I took the accommodating approach because I didn't have any other styles in my tool kit. But pretty soon I realized that I needed to manage conflict from the inside first, by increasing my own self-awareness. And then I started trying to learn how to use some other styles. Once I did that, things improved for me, because I got smarter about conflict.

It really pays to examine your thoughts and feelings about conflict.

It really pays to examine your thoughts and feelings about conflict. One way to do that is to ask yourself some questions. Keeping in mind that there are no "right" responses to these prompts—they're just for self-reflection—think about how you might respond to the following, based on ideas from Robert's book.

- What is conflict?

- How do I usually react to conflict?

- When someone criticizes me or something I have done, I usually . . .

- The best possible outcome of a conflict would be . . .

- When I get angry I usually . . .

- My greatest strength and my greatest weakness in dealing with conflict are . . .

Strive for 60 Seconds of Happiness

For every minute of anger, you lose one minute of happiness. Anger is an emotion that served our ancestors and other animals well. Anger is the mother lion's response when someone or something encroaches on her cub. She immediately gets whatever is threatening the cub to back off. That response works pretty well for a lion, but not so well for a principal.

When you're faced with an unavoidable conflict at work, the chances are great that you're dealing with anger—either your own anger or someone else's. There was a time when we were told to let it all hang out—to vent the anger. However, there is now evidence that releasing the anger only makes the situation worse (Schwartz and McCarthy 2007, 63). It's important to view your anger as a signal that something is not right in your world. But it's just as important to learn to deal with that anger skillfully, because if you don't keep it in check, you could pay a heavy price. One suggestion is to try managing your anger by changing the messages you give to yourself.

Consider the possibility that the anger you're feeling isn't the result of some outside event but that you're making yourself angry. It can be fun to play the blame game when it comes to anger. After all, there's some satisfaction in blaming another person or situation for what's going on. Sometimes it feels good to say "That cafeteria manager made me so mad!" or "Our superintendent is just plain crazy and annoys me so much!" or "That parent is so pushy that it makes me furious!" However, it's better to admit that your anger belongs only to you.

Think about it. When you arrive back at school from a meeting and someone has taken the parking space reserved for you, you react with anger by muttering to yourself, "She really infuriates me!" But the person who took the spot wasn't trying to make you angry. That person was just trying to meet a need of her own—getting a good parking space. You generated the anger, so claim that. Doing so goes a long way toward giving you personal power over the situation. Sometimes, once you recognize that the anger actually came from within you, it can be easier to let go of it. One of the things I often say to myself is "That's not a ditch I want to die in!"

> Consider the possibility that the anger you're feeling isn't the result of some outside event but that you're making yourself angry.

It's Not About You

Have you ever said, "I should not have to put up with this"? That kind of self-talk can prevent you from taking responsibility for your behavior. Ask yourself, "Why not? Is there anything about me that's so special that I don't have to put up with the unfairness and difficulty the role of a leader can bring?" I know you'll answer no. (If you were the type who would answer yes, you wouldn't be reading this book, because you probably wouldn't be in a leadership role.)

Perhaps you should be grateful for all the conflicts you have to deal with. They pay at least half of your salary. If there were no conflicts for a leader to deal with, it would be easy to get someone else to do the work—and for much less pay. If you decide you want a job with more money, then you'll have to expect even more conflict. Don't take conflict so personally. People don't get up in the morning and immediately focus on how they can make you miserable when they get to work. It's not about you!

People don't get up in the morning and immediately focus on how they can make you miserable when they get to work. It's not about you!

Transparency—Not Just for the Overhead Projector

A lot of conflict occurs as a result of a breakdown in communication. So share what's going on. Communicate with others about everything, and make your communication transparent. In other words, be open. That will help you build trust. It will also make it harder for anyone to use a grapevine for anything other than decoration—not as a means of transmitting gossip and rumors.

I remember a time when a group of teachers wanted to team up in a certain way and weren't too happy when I said no. So I made everything transparent. I flooded them with the research data and everything else I could get my hands on to make the case for the approach I felt would serve the students, and not necessarily the teachers, best. I brought everyone in on the communication. I figured that way, if they were using the parking lot to talk about the issue in a negative way, at least everyone would know where I was coming from and could make up his or her own mind.

In Every Adversity, There's a Seed of Opportunity

A number of years ago, my husband worked with George Ballas, the man who invented the Weed Eater string trimmer. Mr. Ballas always used to tell my husband that in every adversity, there is a seed of opportunity. You just have to look for it.

The Weed Eater is a good example of this. Years ago, Mr. Ballas was in the real estate business in Houston, and things were not going well for him at all. He knew he'd have to do something in order to survive and provide for his wife and five children. At the same time, Mr. Ballas had been having a hard time removing the weeds from around the trees in his yard. That adversity actually afforded him an opportunity. Thinking that others might be frustrated by the same problem, he decided to try to find a better way to deal with the weeds. He persevered until he came up with something that worked: he took an old popcorn can and a piece of string, and he built an early prototype of the Weed Eater. The rest is history.

I often think about that when I'm going through a change or faced with a conflict or adversity. There is always some danger, some fear, but there is also a hidden opportunity. You can help yourself and others negotiate through those difficult times when you look for the opportunities that changes and conflicts present.

A Tool for Managing Conflict

THE HAND DANCE

Purpose:

> This is one of my favorite activities to use with teachers because it's a fun way to let them experience different ways of handling conflict. It's adapted from an activity that appears in *Person to Person,* by John F. Taylor.

Materials:

> None

Time:

> 15 minutes

Procedure:

1. Ask teachers to stand up and pair off, then decide which partner will be A and which will be B.

2. Ask them to face each other and extend their arms so that their palms are touching.

3. Tell them that they will now do a hand dance. Explain that a hand dance is always graceful. To start the hand dance, instruct Partner A to begin to move her hands in a slow and graceful motion. Tell them that A is the leader for the dance and B is the follower. Tell B to exert no more pressure on A's hands than is necessary to follow her lead.

4. Announce that B should now begin to ask permission from A to be the leader. However, each time B asks, A is to deny him permission and give him a put-down. If you want, you can provide responses for A to give to her partner. For example, you might tell A to say, "I am your boss. I will always be your boss. You must always do as I say. You just breathe, and I will do the rest."

5. After a couple of minutes, call time and announce that this part of the hand dance is over. Ask teachers how they

would label this way of handling conflict. They should say that it's autocratic or domineering.

6. Now ask them to start a new hand dance, with A still the leader and B still the follower. Ask B once again to request permission to be the leader and A to again deny that request and give B a put-down. In other words, this part is exactly the same as the first round, except that this time you're not providing a specific prompt.

7. After a couple of minutes, announce in a loud voice, "B, this is your chance. Take over the lead." Things will get rowdy now, because B will get out of control. That's when you tell them loudly, "Remember to stay graceful."

8. Call time and announce that this part of the hand dance is over. Ask participants how they might label this way of handling conflict. They should say something like "All out war!" Ask them if you told them to struggle. When they say no, remind them that this is what usually happens when someone is dominated—the person being dominated wants to fight back.

9. Now ask the partners to lean forward with their palms touching and move their feet back as far as they can without falling. Tell them this is a conflict that is deadlocked.

10. Challenge them to hand dance in this deadlocked position. They will not be able to do it.

11. Ask them to come out of their deadlocked position without letting go of each other's hands.

12. Ask them in what direction they had to move in order to come out of the deadlocked position. They will say closer

together. Point out that to solve a deadlocked conflict, people must work together.

13. Ask participants to start hand dancing again, but this time to trade the lead back and forth.

14. After a couple of minutes, announce that the hand dance is over. Ask the group for ways to label this last way of dealing with conflict. They will say collaborative. Tell them that cooperation in a conflict is like a dance that draws people together.

A Pearl to Ponder

A crisis is a terrible thing to waste.

—Paul Romer

Secret #6

Emotional Minefields:
Setting Boundaries

Back when I was a new principal, my phone rang at 5:30 one Monday morning. It was a teacher who didn't live far from me. She told me that over the weekend, she'd had car problems and had left her car at a repair shop. She wondered if I could give her a ride to school every morning that week while the car was being repaired. I really didn't want to do that because I had some off-site meetings during the week and dropping her at school each morning would mean going way out of my way. However, I told her that of course I would be happy to give her a ride. So I picked her up, and we went to school. I was resentful but pretended to be my typical cheerful, accommodating self.

The minute I got to school that day, I was greeted by a teacher with a wad of tissue weeping at my door. It was very early in the morning, and I had really been looking forward to returning some phone calls and catching up on reading some memos. (Thank goodness we didn't have fax machines, e-mail, or cell phones then, or I probably would have had a major meltdown.) She told me that she was in the middle of a personal crisis and needed to talk to me. She said that her husband had left her the night before. She was devastated and by that time crying uncontrollably. I started to cry with her—*really* cry with her. She was in crisis, and I was in crisis with her, before the bell had even rung to start school. I was being empathetic to her situation, but because I did not have clear boundaries, I had also "caught" her "cold" (her emotions).

> She was in crisis, and I was in crisis with her, before the bell had even rung to start school.

The whole day went pretty much that way. I felt as if I was going from one war zone to another, stepping in one emotional minefield after another. At the end of the day, when I loaded up my bag to leave, it was so heavy with all the paperwork and tasks I hadn't finished during the day that it caused the seat belt alarm to sound in my car. I literally had a lot of baggage with me! By the time I got home, about fourteen hours after I'd arrived at school, I had given and given and given to others all day long, and I was given out. It took me a while to unwind, and then all I could do was fall into bed to get a few hours' sleep before I had to do it all over again.

After a few months of this, I made a fascinating discovery about being a principal. My son was involved in baseball at the time and was in a highly competitive environment. I watched how he worked out and the sacrifices he made to be a great player. One evening while watching one of his games, I decided that the stresses and demands I was facing each day were far greater than anything even a professional athlete could possibly understand. If my son were to strike out in the bottom of the ninth, the other team would win. I knew that would stress him out. His muscles would tense up, his heart rate would increase, and those stress hormones that produce anxiety would be released. However, that classic stress response would subside after the game ended. The slate would be wiped clean. There would be another game in a few days, and he'd have a chance to redeem himself.

"But I don't get that chance," I thought. I felt that I lived with that typical stress response all day long—my muscles were tense, my heart raced, and I was anxious all the time. The difference between my stress and my son's was that mine never subsided. Why couldn't I go home each evening with more of a feeling of well-being? Maybe a Valium salt lick in my office would help!

Then I realized something: emotions really run the show. If I could get better control of my emotions, I could bring to life the talent and skills I possessed. If not, I would be constantly stepping into those emotional minefields at work and would be left with a stress response that wouldn't quit. But how could I get better control of my emotions?

A clearer sense of my boundaries would have helped, but I was too clueless even to know I *needed* boundaries. For instance, in my response to the early-morning phone call from my neighbor, I was empathetic to her, understanding her situation with the car, but I was not empathetic to myself. Then I was angry with myself because I had not been assertive with her. I could have taken better care of myself had I maintained clearer boundaries.

When I arrived at school and was drawn into the crisis of the crying teacher, my problems continued because I "caught" that teacher's feelings. It was important to be empathetic to her family situation, but a more objective approach would have been more helpful to her.

This doesn't mean that I should have been cold and indifferent to her situation. It means that as the EGO (emotional guide for others), I needed to help her continue to function even in the midst of her personal crisis. If I had it to do over again, I might have let her leave early, but I might also have encouraged her to first teach her class that day. I could have helped her see that it's possible to put a crisis aside for a period of time and still function.

> I needed to help her continue to function even in the midst of her personal crisis.

I realize now that if I had kept my boundaries that day, *I* could have been more functional as well. But no, I fell into the emotional minefield. A poor sense of boundaries was affecting my life as a principal.

That brings me to the sixth secret of motivating and inspiring people: setting boundaries. Let's look at what is meant by boundaries and at how maintaining boundaries can help you be a more assertive and effective leader.

The dictionary definition of a boundary is something that indicates a border or limit. Baseball players stay within the boundaries of the baselines when running from one base to another. NASCAR drivers stay within the lines on the track. Ballroom dancers perform to the rhythm and tempo of the music. All three groups acknowledge the boundaries that have been set to govern their behavior.

Think of the fence between your yard and your neighbor's. That's a physical boundary that separates your land from your neighbor's. Just as your neighbor might get angry if you jumped the fence and trespassed on his land, problems can occur when others trespass on our personal or emotional property. If you don't know what your boundaries are, you certainly can't enforce them! It's possible to improve many stressful situations at work just by becoming aware of and enforcing your boundaries. In fact, boundaries establish a framework for achieving your personal best.

Boundaries are an imaginary line of protection that you draw around yourself. Strong personal boundaries are not walls that isolate. They don't mean that you're cold and unfeeling. On the contrary, maintaining your personal boundaries can result in increased trust and respect—both the respect you have for yourself and the respect others have for you.

Often the problems you experience in the people part of your job are related to boundaries. There will always be someone you deal with on a daily basis who is a bully, an intimidator, a gossip, a complainer, or a know-it-all—in short, someone who drives you crazy! You probably dream of the day when you won't have to deal with this person anymore. Dream on. It's not going to happen. That's life—the life of a leader. If you change jobs, you'll find new difficult people on the new job.

It's easy to blame others in this situation. How many times have you said, "If only that parent weren't so pushy" or "If she would just listen during faculty meetings instead of talking to the person next to her, everything would run so much more smoothly"? But boundary problems are not really about the other person; they're about you. It all comes down to how you respond to that challenging person. Regardless of how he is behaving, you can establish healthy boundaries.

But boundary problems are not really about the other person; they're about you.

Maintaining your own boundaries not only helps you function better but also helps you help the people around you. When you become more tolerant of others and less defensive, the rest of the school will follow suit. You'll be able to avoid those emotional minefields and to help others avoid them, too.

Let's explore ways to think about boundaries. Try this experiment: close your eyes and think of the word "boundary." What picture do you see? Do you see a wall? That's what most people see. However, I'm going to ask you to consider thinking of boundaries in a different way. I'd like to suggest that you think of a boundary as the membrane of a living cell. If you were to look at a cell under a microscope, you'd see that its membrane is not continuous. It has "windows," or receptors, each of which has a kind of guard that says "You can come in" or "You can go out." The membrane of the cell functions well because it lets certain things in and allows other things out. This is an example of a flexible boundary.

Now let's look at boundary issues in terms of the Human Doings and Human Beings approaches.

The Human Doings Approach

This approach involves a couple of boundary problems. The first is that it typically involves thinking of boundaries as rigid, thick walls. That type of boundary—the "my way or the highway" approach—is not open to input or influence from others. Teachers who work with leaders and boundaries like this often feel as if they're banging their heads against those walls, because they feel that their ideas aren't listened to. This type of inflexibility on the leader's part kills innovation, because teachers say, "Why should I work on this? He'll never go for it."

Another kind of dysfunctional boundary is like a cell in which the membranes are weak, and the cells share boundaries; they'll accept anything that comes their way. If you have this kind of boundaries, you are too open and eager to please, and you end up letting other people take control. You can become so accommodating that you lose your sense of self and might even get depressed. You start to feel trapped in a bad situation. That's how I was feeling my first year as a principal, when I was so clueless about boundaries.

And the situation tends to get worse, because this approach can drain your energy and leave you stuck in a world of perceived urgency.

The Human Beings Approach

Now consider a third possibility. Think of this approach as being like a cell in which the membranes are flexible and porous, but they're firm when they need to be. If one cell said to another, "Give me your nucleus," the other cell would not do that, because giving away its nucleus would kill it. This is an example of functional boundaries. It illustrates taking a stand, not building a wall. If you have this type of boundaries, you're open to others' ideas and opinions and willing to negotiate, but sometimes you also say to yourself, "If I compromise on this issue, I will lose my sense of integrity or morals. This is nonnegotiable." You stand firm on certain key issues and keep your sense of self, while still being flexible and open to the ideas of others. With this approach, you don't try to control others or think you know the only way to accomplish something. You don't get stuck in stubbornness or a negative attitude. Instead, you actively listen to a request or the issues involved in a conflict, and you respond in an assertive and functional manner.

"Assertiveness" is not a synonym for "aggression." The intent of aggressive communication is to get your own way and to dominate others. When someone is aggressive, she is insensitive to the rights and needs of others; she communicates in ways that demean, humiliate, or coerce.

Nonassertiveness goes to the other extreme. The intent of nonassertive behavior is to avoid conflict altogether. This usually means that your wishes are subordinated to the wishes of others. You don't tell others what you're thinking or what you want. That allows them to choose for you and potentially to infringe on your boundaries. The intent of assertiveness is to communicate honestly and directly. When you're assertive, you make choices for yourself without harming or being harmed by others.

This is an example of functional boundaries. It illustrates taking a stand, not building a wall.

Not only must you know yourself and your own boundaries, but since you're in charge of the school, you must think about the school's boundaries, too. When you clarify your position on a given subject, as well as the school's position on that subject, you're setting boundaries. You're also inspiring others to maintain their boundaries and to decide what is most important to them. In this way, you're helping them function better—not only individually but also as a group. That's what the Human Beings approach is all about.

Tips for Setting Boundaries

Give a Positive No

Do you remember the book *Getting to Yes*, which I spoke about as part of secret number 5? William Ury, a coauthor of that book, also wrote a book called *The Power of a Positive No*. In *The Power of a Positive No*, he gives a simple three-step method for saying no in any situation and, at the same time, saying yes to what counts for you—your needs, priorities, and boundaries. His three-step approach is "Yes! No. Yes?" The first yes is saying yes to yourself and what matters to you. The no is stating your boundary. The second yes is an invitation to the other person to protect and honor the relationship. As Ury says, this method helps you stand on your own two feet and not on another's toes (Ury 2007, 17)!

Let's look at a way to apply this approach in a school setting. Suppose a parent interrupts a conversation you're having with a teacher in the hallway. In this case, the first yes isn't even stated out loud. Instead, you just mentally say  yes to yourself—affirming in your own mind that you don't want to stop talking to the teacher and that the parent needs to wait. Then comes the no: in a respectful way, you tell the parent that you are in the middle of something. You immediately follow up with the second yes, explaining that if the parent will go to the front office and sign in, you'll be there as soon as possible. That final yes is the invitation to the parent to follow proper procedures for visitors in the building and to wait until you can meet with her.

Move Beyond Fear

It takes courage to set a boundary, maintain it, and communicate it. Lots of times when someone sets boundaries that are too rigid, the reason they do that is fear. Someone who's afraid to trust others, for example, can lose the empathy and compassion that are so much a part of the Human Beings approach to leadership. Someone who's afraid of conflict or rejection tends to set up inflexible boundaries. To have a better chance of establishing functional boundaries, you have to change your behavior. You can't just wake up one morning and tell yourself 50 times that today you will set and maintain more appropriate boundaries. Nope, not that easy. It might be really difficult to send that e-mail that involves communicating your needs assertively. Changing behavior takes courage and practice. But that's the only way you can get better at those emotional minefields.

Three Can Be a Crowd

Sometimes when you're not comfortable dealing with boundaries, you end up pulling in a third person to help you resolve things. Though you may not be consciously thinking in these terms, you're trying to diffuse the tension. The problem is that this "triangling" can actually lead to a lot *more* tension in the relationship because now there are three people involved and the tension can shift around. What begins as an attempt to resolve the situation—bringing in another person—usually ends up just making the situation worse.

Let me give you an example. Once I had a very angry parent in my office. She was upset because she felt that her daughter was being treated unfairly. I didn't agree with her and was feeling annoyed and frustrated with the disrespectful way she was speaking to me. She was demanding that I take certain actions and take them immediately. (Sound familiar? I told you there aren't a lot of difficult people. They just move around a lot. You've met with the same parent before, haven't you?)

So here we had a two-person relationship (the parent and me) that was becoming increasingly unstable. The tension was high. The parent's way of dealing with that was to demand that I bring in the superintendent, which would create a triangle. She tried to threaten me by telling me that if I didn't do what she wanted, she would call him. (She used his first name to impress on me the fact that they were friends.) She was trying to break through the boundary I had set for myself—that I wouldn't negotiate with her on her demands. However, I stood firm. In fact, I told her that I'd be glad to give her the superintendent's phone number if she didn't have it with her. (Obviously, this incident occurred in my later years as a principal, when I had a better sense of my boundaries and how to communicate them.)

Now wouldn't the world be a better place if we could always be with-it enough to realize when someone else is "triangling," if we could just say, "Oh, dear! Looks like we have a triangle here. What can we do to fix this situation?" That isn't easy to do, because triangles are driven by emotion, not logic. But we can start by being aware of triangles and by watching for them in our own communication and the communication of others.

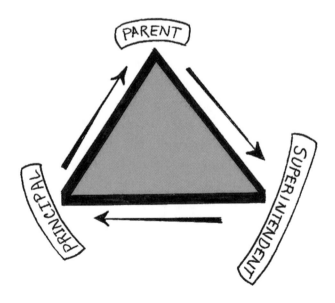

Uncommon Leadership in Education

Tools for Setting Boundaries

FIGURING OUT YOUR BOUNDARIES

Purpose:

Often as a leader, you're moving at such a furious pace that you don't have time to stop and ask yourself what you stand for and who you want to be. When that happens, external demands end up dictating all your actions. This exercise can help you figure out what's important to you and then set appropriate boundaries.

Materials:

Graphic organizer (see illustration)

Time:

Varies; it could be something you'll want to think about over an extended period of time

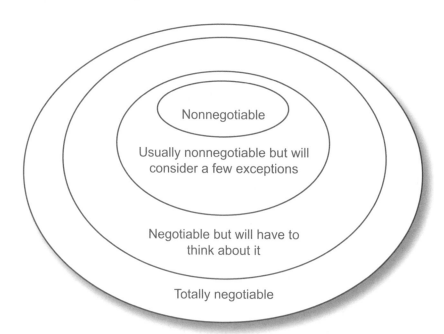

Nonnegotiable

Usually nonnegotiable but will consider a few exceptions

Negotiable but will have to think about it

Totally negotiable

Procedure:

1. Look at the graphic organizer.
The inner circle represents your
nonnegotiable issues. Remember that
everyone's boundaries are different,
so what is nonnegotiable for you might
not be nonnegotiable for someone else. For example, if
a parent was driving me nuts and all I wanted was for
that person to disappear, I wouldn't hire a hit man to get
rid of her (not that I might not think about it). That is a
nonnegotiable issue for me.

Nonnegotiable

2. The next circle represents
things that are nonnego-
tiable but for which you're
willing to make a few exceptions. You would probably
put "no stealing" and "no lying"
in your nonnegotiable circle, but there might be circumstances in which you'd make exceptions. You might consider stealing a piece of bread to feed a child who would
starve to death without it. And what about lying? Well,
I remember a time when a young teacher in our district
was diagnosed with a terminal illness. She had two very
young children. The doctor knew the prognosis was not
good, but instead of telling her she had only a few months
to live, he softened his explanation with what we call a
"little white lie," telling her that new discoveries were being made all the time to cure her disease.

Usually nonnegotiable but will
consider a few exceptions

3. The next circle represents
most of the issues that
you deal with in your
day-to-day life. These
issues are negotiable,
but only after you've
really thought about what
you're being asked to do. You
might be willing to make an exception to your general
rule, but you might not be willing to go as far as someone
is asking you to. Usually the things that fall in this circle
have something to do with time limits. If you're a parent,

Negotiable but will have to
think about it

think of the times you've said something like this to your teenager: "Yes, you can stay out until 1:00 a.m., but you must call and check in with me at midnight." I remember having a teacher on my staff who wanted to attend an early-morning service at her church for one week. It would mean that she might be a few minutes late getting to school each morning. Since it was only for a week, I went along with her request. The issue was negotiable for me.

4. The last circle represents all those things that are totally open to negotiation. You're perfectly willing to go along with the other person's preferences on these issues because the issues just aren't that important to you. For example, if the secretary asks you whether you want the office computer in this corner or another corner, you're happy to leave the decision up to the secretary, because you don't really care where it goes.

Totally negotiable

5. Spend time thinking about what you would put in the different circles. You're not born with this knowledge; you have to figure it out for yourself. So many times, we just follow rules and regulations that have already been established. We don't really think about those rules; we don't review them and define them in terms of our own priorities. As a result, we may end up with poor boundaries.

6. Consider going through this exercise with your teachers to help them set priorities, too. For example, let's say that the students at your school wear uniforms. The uniform for girls is a skirt. But one especially cold and wintry day, one girl wears pants to school. The girl's teacher comes to you very upset and wants to send her home immediately. You might help the teacher understand that this is not that big a deal and can be dealt with in a better way. In other words, you can teach the teacher to be less rigid and more flexible.

COMMUNICATING A BOUNDARY

Purpose:

This exercise provides a framework for you to use when communicating a boundary.

Materials:

None

Time:

Not much longer than the amount of time it would take not to communicate

Procedure:

1. Use the ASAP approach:

   - A = Acknowledge the other person's wishes, needs, and feelings.

   - S = State your boundary.

   - A = Assert yourself.

   - P = Present an alternative.

2. Let's apply this tool to the situation I told you about earlier—the one in which the teacher wanted a ride from me to school every day. I could have given a better response, reflecting clearer boundaries on my part, if I'd said, "I bet it's such a pain to have a car in the repair shop. [Acknowledge the teacher's feelings.] I can't pick you up and take you to work every day this week. [State

your boundary in an assertive manner.] I can come by on Wednesday morning, though. [Present an alternative.]

USING ASAP WITH STUDENTS

Purpose:

This communication sequence can help you offer students choices for behavior.

Materials:

None

Time:

A couple of seconds

Procedure:

1. Follow the procedure described in the preceding tool, using these guidelines:

   - A = Acknowledge the student's wishes, needs, and feelings.

   - S = State your boundary.

   - A = Assert yourself.

   - P = Present choices.

2. For example, let's say a student in a kindergarten classroom is using modeling clay at a center and decides to eat the clay. Using ASAP, you might say something like this to the student: "I can tell you must be hungry. [Acknowledge the student's need.] However, clay is not for eating. [State your boundary in an assertive manner.] You need to stop eating it now or leave the center. You decide." [Present choices.]

3. Here's another example. If an older student is being disrespectful, you might say, "I can tell you're angry with me. [Acknowledge the student's feelings.] However, I will not be talked to that way. [State your boundary in an assertive manner.] I will be glad to talk with you when your voice sounds like mine, or we can agree to talk later—perhaps after school. You decide." [Present choices.]

A Pearl to Ponder

Everything can be taken from a man but one thing: the last of the human freedoms—to choose one's attitude in any given set of circumstances, to choose one's own way.

—Viktor Frankl

Secret #7

Know Thyself: Maintaining Your Motivation

At a time when the economy was not in the greatest shape, a man in Houston was laid off. He needed to find work quickly because he had a wife and children to support. One day while reading the local newspaper, he noticed that there was an opening at the Houston Zoo. He immediately called and informed the human resources department that he was an accountant and would be happy to work for them. The human resources director told him that they didn't need an accountant. What they needed was a gorilla. Yes, you read that right—a gorilla.

The director explained that the real gorilla had died and they needed someone to dress up and be their gorilla while they were waiting for the real gorilla (the new one) to arrive. The accountant laughed and said, "You've got to be kidding me. I'm not going to do anything as crazy as that." To which the human resources person replied, "Well, it pays $200 per day. Take it or leave it." The accountant then began to think that no one would know it was him, so he decided to take the job just until the real gorilla arrived.

It took three people to get the man in the gorilla suit, but eventually there he was, crouching in the gorilla's cage and feeling totally humiliated. Then when some children and their parents arrived, he decided he should start acting like a gorilla. Before long, a crowd had gathered, and they all had their cameras out and were taking pictures. He decided that if he could swing from a vine hanging in the cage, he would really give the crowd a thrill. But just as he was about to try the stunt, he slipped from the vine and fell into the cage next to his. It was the lion's den!

He grabbed the bars of the lion's den and started shouting madly, "I'm a man! I'm a man! I'm not a gorilla!" He was shouting louder and louder as the lion crept closer and closer to him. He was sure he was just about to take his last breath when he heard the lion say, "Shut up, or you'll get us both fired!"

"Shut up, or you'll get us both fired!"

Okay, that was a pathetic joke, I know. But think about it. You could get fired from your job. You could even get fired from being a husband or wife or sister or brother. But you can't get fired from being you!

If it's true that uncommon leadership involves inspiring and influencing the best in others, it only makes sense that managing your own motivation needs to become one of your top priorities. And that's secret number seven.

Tips for Maintaining Motivation
Engage Your Passion

I doubt very seriously that you love everything you do at work. I know that when I was a principal, I didn't bound out of bed in the morning because I was so excited about the IEP meetings I had scheduled that day that I just couldn't wait to get to school. But I'm sure there are things that you are passionate about—things that you do best, that tap into your talents, and that give you the most enjoyment. Ask yourself what you do best and what you enjoy the most, then try to establish a schedule that encourages you to do more of those things on a regular basis.

For example, I always felt the most effective, absorbed, inspired, and fulfilled when I could brainstorm new ideas for teachers and then share those ideas. I could not get excited about schedules or reading reports or analyzing data. But my assistant principal just loved being surrounded by that stuff. It was a match made in heaven. She carved out time to work with the reports, and I carved out time to work on brainstorming. Certainly, we couldn't devote all our time and energy to our respective passions every day, but we got pretty good at pursuing our passions often enough to help keep us inspired and motivated. Identify those things that bring you pleasure at work and find ways to spend time on them!

Give Yourself Permission to Be Good Enough

Beware of falling into the trap of trying to be perfect. Because leaders are usually high achievers, they often strive for perfection. If you're a perfectionist, you probably repeat the "I should have . . ." message to yourself all day. You may say, "I should have visited that teacher's room today"; "I should have finished that write-up before I left for the meeting"; "I should have the agenda ready by now." Your whole day turns into a constant recitation of "I should have, I should have, I should have. . . ." It's not always easy, but I'd suggest that you really focus on avoiding the "should have" trap. In other words, give yourself permission to be human.

Express Gratitude Whenever You Can

One year our assistant superintendent lost her husband very suddenly. At the first principals' meeting after she returned to work, before she addressed any agenda items, she asked each of us to pair off with the principal in the room who was our "best buddy." She asked us to sit face-to-face and spend a minute or two expressing appreciation for all the things that person did. She told us that we needed to remember that we live very busy and hurried lives, and although we often take time to give negative attention to others, we usually don't take time to give positive attention to the people in our lives who count the most. She encouraged us to do more of that, because as she had learned in a tragic way, you never know when those people might be gone.

Think of someone connected with your school—a student, teacher, staff member, or parent—to whom you are grateful. As soon as you finish reading this, take a few minutes to express your gratitude to that person. The communication could take the form of an e-mail, a note, a phone call, or a face-to-face conversation. Believe me, you will benefit just as much as, if not more than, the person you acknowledge.

Practice Saying "Thank You"

What do you usually do when someone gives you a compliment? Let's say someone says that she likes your jacket. Do you respond by saying "Oh, this is old. I got it on sale"? Instead, practice just saying "Thank you." Appreciate the positive attention; you probably don't get it that often.

Would you like to know the graduate level of accepting a compliment? The next time your boss tells you that you did a great job on some report, say, "Thank you, and exactly what about that report did you like?" (That's called "milking it for all that it's worth.")

Create New Stories

Once a month, I get together with my girlfriends. I have known these four women since our children were little, because our boys grew up playing baseball together. We spent hours and hours, weeks and weeks, years and years bonding with one another at our kids' practices and games. Even though our boys are grown up now, we've maintained our friendship and look forward to our monthly get-togethers.

Now at some point over the years, those women and I made a promise to ourselves. We agreed that if, at any one of our meetings, we started reminiscing about all the ballpark stories and experiences we had when our kids were young, that would mean we'd run out of new experiences. We needed to create new stories! So we decided that each of us would have to come up with a new experience to share at every meeting. I honestly think this practice has been good for our emotional health, and I highly recommend that you try something similar in your own life. Don't ever stop creating new stories.

I highly recommend that you try something similar in your own life. Don't ever stop creating new stories.

Fake It 'Til You Make It

When you put this book down in a couple of minutes, stand up, smile, hold your head up high, and walk with brisk strides wherever you are headed next. Looking like you're enthusiastic and motivated will help you feel that way, and others will respond to you in kind.

That Last Look in the Mirror

Each morning, right before you leave for work, glance at yourself in the mirror. Reflect on an accomplishment. Enjoy the satisfaction of attaining that goal for just a minute. Then say aloud, "_____ [the name of your school or district], you are darn lucky I'm showing up today!"

There's Something About Enthusiasm

One Friday afternoon, one of our kindergarten teachers told her students that first thing on Monday morning, they would have show-and-tell. So on Monday morning, one of her students, Johnny, was madly waving his hand in the air for her to call on him. He had something important to tell. He walked to the front of the class and told everyone that on Saturday, he and his dad had gone on a fishing trip, and each had caught 75 fish, each one weighing 75 pounds.

The teacher looked at Johnny in disbelief. She said to him, "Would you believe me if I told you that on my way to school this morning, a big old grizzly bear came out from behind a bush and was just about to grab me, when a little bitty puppy dog came out and grabbed the bear, slung him back and forth, and saved my life?"

Johnny promptly replied, "Yes, ma'am, because that was my dog!"

There is something about enthusiasm! Nothing great was ever accomplished without it. I suggest to you that a certain amount of excessive enthusiasm is a necessary trait for all uncommon leaders.

A Tool for Maintaining Motivation

THE CORNER PEOPLE

Purpose:

> This activity will help you to focus on people who have inspired and influenced you.

Materials:

> Paper and pen or pencil

Time:

> As long as you need or want

Procedure:

1. Imagine a boxing ring with a person in each corner. The people in the corners are your "corner people"—the four people who have influenced your life the most. They are the ones who have most inspired and motivated you and helped make you who you are.

2. Draw the boxing ring on your paper, then draw a stick figure in each corner. Write the name of one of your corner people next to each stick figure.

3. Think about each person and write next to that person's name one word or phrase that expresses a gift that person gave you. For example, you might write the word "courage" next to the name of someone who gave you the courage to face the tasks and demands of your job.

4. Frequently visit this piece of paper, because one way you can keep your motivation high is to reflect on and remember those who have helped you. Your mind needs rejuvenation from time to time. When you get discouraged dealing with the people issues, step back and remind yourself that there is no more noble profession in the world than one that involves helping another human being succeed. This is really what your teachers want from you: help and support in creating their own success. And that's what the Human Beings approach is all about.

A Pearl to Ponder

Inspiring others is a matter of attitude, not just aptitude.

—Betty Hollas

A Closing Comment

My hope is that you will consider some of the suggestions you've read in this book. I think that if you try to practice these ideas, you, as an uncommon leader, will be able to create an atmosphere in which teachers will feel good about themselves, one in which they'll feel energized and motivated to do their best. This will spill over to the students as the teachers inspire their students to do their best every day. The end result will be an environment in which students and adults alike are more empathetic toward one another and at the same time establish clearer boundaries; an environment in which there's less aggression and more collaboration; an environment in which everyone in the school community makes a greater effort together than each person could have made alone.

Academic rigor will not be sacrificed. Quite the opposite will be true. You will be helping your teachers to fulfill their main mission: teaching. You will be helping your students fulfill their main mission: learning. And you will have fulfilled *your* main mission: inspiring everyone to do his or her best.

Resources

Albert, Linda. 1996. *Cooperative discipline inplementation guide*. Circle Pines, Minnesota: American Guidance Service.

Crum, Thomas. 1987. *The magic of conflict*. New York: Simon and Schuster.

Fisher, Roger, William Ury, and Bruce Patton. 2003. *Getting to yes*. New York: Random House Business Books.

Fullan, Michael. 2008. *The six secrets of change: What the best leaders do to help their organizations survive and thrive*. San Francisco: Jossey-Bass.

Goleman, Daniel. 1995. *Emotional intelligence*. New York: Bantam Books.

————. 2002. Leadership that gets results. *Harvard Business Review* 78 (March–April): 78–90.

————. 2006. *Social intelligence: The new science of human relationships*. New York: Bantam Books.

Goleman, Daniel, Richard Boyatzis, and Annie McKee. 2002. *Primal leadership: Realizing the power of emotional intelligence*. Boston: Harvard Business School Press.

Maslow, Abraham. 1998. *Maslow on management*. New York: John Wiley and Sons.

Menninger, Walter W. 1988. Adaptation and morale: Predictable responses to life change. *Bulletin of the Menninger Clinic* 52: 198–210.

Robert, Marc. 1982. *Managing conflict from the inside out*. San Diego: Pfeiffer.

Salovey, Peter, and John Mayer. 1990. Emotional intelligence. *Imagination, Cognition, and Personality* 9: 185–211.

Schwartz, Tony, and Catherine McCarthy. 2007. Manage your energy, not your time. *Harvard Business Review,* October, 63–73.

Taylor, John F. 1984. *Person to person.* Saratoga, CA: R & E.

Ury, William. 2007. *The power of a positive no.* New York: Bantam Books.

Index

Also by Betty Hollas

Differentiated Instruction (with Char Forsten and Jim Grant)

Differentiated Textbooks (with Char Forsten and Jim Grant)

Differentiating Instruction in a Whole-Group Setting (3–8)

Differentiating Instruction in a Whole-Group Setting (7–12)

Question-Answer Relationships (QAR)

6 Ways to Teach the 6 Traits of Writing

Bring Betty Hollas right to your school
for on-site training!
To learn how, call 877-388-2054.